SHINE!

————— ❧❧❧❧ —————

Inspirational Stories of Choosing Success Over Adversity

Prominence Publishing

Published by Prominence Publishing.

For information visit www.prominencepublishing.com

Cover design by Prominence Publishing.

ISBN: 978-0-9958274-5-5

First Edition: April 2017

Table of Contents

Introduction

Successful women are often perceived as "lucky." Back in 2002, when I started experiencing financial success with my business, I said to one of my mentors, "I feel so lucky. I can't believe this is happening." And he replied with a famous quote by Thomas Jefferson, "Suzanne, the harder you work, the luckier you get." I learned that to get what I wanted, I would need to work hard. I thought that if I just worked hard, success would come and everything else would take care of itself.

What I didn't see coming was overwhelming periods of adversity. The trouble is, you *never* see them coming! Sometimes the craziest thing can come out of the blue and completely throw you off track. It's how you react to it that makes all the difference. Will you let it bring you down, and cause you to give up? Or will it make you stronger and more determined to succeed?

I wanted to compile and publish this interview-style book featuring successful women entrepreneurs as a ray of hope for others who may be experiencing adversity. The 10 women selected for this book were interviewed and asked similar questions. Their answers are diverse, inspiring and enlightening!

Every woman featured in this book is a beautiful example of success and each one has been through some tough times.

You will notice two important points that are a recurring pattern: one – often the period of adversity lasted for <u>years</u>, and two – it's how she reacted that made all the difference. The bottom line is that they never gave up!

Each co-author offers tips on how to overcome adversity and explains the importance of having a positive mindset.

Successful women are not simply people who have had it easy. They are the ones who have fought tooth and nail to get where they are; they've been pushed down, stepped on and stepped over, and have come back again with their heads held high.

The bottom line is this: **Do Not Give Up.** I say this to my kids and my clients constantly. **Do Not Give Up.** So many people work and work and work and then right before they succeed, they give up.

I sincerely hope that you glean wisdom and insight from SHINE and I wish you much success in business and life.

To your success,

Suzanne Doyle-Ingram
Publisher
Prominence Publishing

Chapter 1:

She Who Dares Wins

By Maureen (Mo) Hagan

Mo Hagan shares her story of how she pursued and shaped her own success as a global fitness ambassador despite being told that such a career in health and fitness did not exist and that she should not set her dreams on such a grandiose scale. Academically, Mo was not the smartest student. Athletically, Mo was not strong or fast enough. And while Mo lacked the skills and self-confidence at times, she leveraged her natural ability to see a vision for her life, the passion and perseverance to withstand rejection and pursue her dreams, and the posture to stand up against rejection and negative influencers. Instead, Mo powered up her natural high energy and 'never-quit' attitude and practiced harder and longer than most of her teammates on sports teams in high-school and university, and over time she cultivated a level of confidence and self-belief, not to mention disciplined learning habits.

Mo is the Vice President of Program Innovation at GoodLife Fitness and canfitpro.

My Early Years

Although hyperactive as a child, my first structured experience with fitness was thanks to my high school teacher, Mrs. Ellie Armstrong. She taught me that one doesn't have to be good at sports to participate, and to train for sheer joy and for the benefits that fitness paid. She always inspired me to work toward achieving my own goal, not the goal of the team. If I made the team – great! But, as long as I improved and personally grew as a result of the training & experience, I was truly a winner. As it turned out, I was cut from almost every team that I tried out for in high school (except for cross-country running, gymnastics and cheerleading).

I graduated from high school with a passion for running, exercise of every sort and a career goal of doing "anything to do with fitness." It has always been my passion and my purpose to inspire and help others. Leading, teaching and positively influencing people is my calling and I'm proud to serve the world in this way. Through career counseling in high school, I soon learned that I could make a career out of my passion for physical activity and although it wasn't my dream to teach physical education I pursued my passion.

While there were no specific careers in fitness, per se, aerobic dance exercise began to emerge in the early 1980s at the same time I was attending Western University for Physical Health Education and Physiotherapy. After 6 years of university I graduated and landed what I thought was my dream career as a physiotherapist at University Hospital in London, Ontario. After a few years, I decided to take a leave of absence, and travel to the South Pacific and Asia to fulfill my dream of seeing that part of the world. That trip changed my life and my career forever. Immediately upon my return, I was offered a leadership position at GoodLife Fitness and I resigned as a physiotherapist (although I am still licensed to practice to this day).

When I told my mother I was resigning from my job where I was secure in salary and long term benefits, to take on this new position at GoodLife, not yet defined and without any benefits or security, she said, "Mo, you aren't really going to quit your job to become an aerobics instructor for the rest of your life, are you?" to which I replied, "Oh yes I am, and I plan to take it to the top and build myself a career that allows me to teach and train instructors and share my passion for helping people become healthier through fitness." I never looked back and despite what everyone advised, I made it the top of the fitness industry. Without realizing it, I created my dream career and I'm happy and fulfilled with my decision today!

Going Through Times of Adversity

As cliché as it sounds, a defining moment of adversity in my life occurred the day I was born.

My mother found out the night before that she was going to have twins and having only gained 15 pounds with her pregnancy, we were a high-risk delivery. Although I was first born, I was the smallest. I was very tiny, weighing less than 3 pounds.

My mother was told by her doctors that I would be the weaker one and likely to struggle with my health for a good part of my life. I was in the preemie neonatal unit much longer than my sister. I was a bit delayed in my growth and motor development, and required various therapies. I also had a hip dysplasia that caused me to walk incorrectly. My mother was not satisfied with the standard care for this condition, or the 'wait and see' attitude from my doctor, so she asked to be referred to a specialist and insisted that I wear braces on my legs to help me learn to walk correctly. While I do not remember a lot about that time, my mother said that when I started to walk, there was no turning back. I ran!

My mother believed that I must have heard my doctors' diagnosis and was determined to prove everyone wrong, and I did. Interestingly enough, I grew to surpass my sister Pauline in bodyweight and height and was often introduced to my grandmother's friends as "the bigger one of the two."

My mother was really determined that I would be independent, even though I was a twin; she wanted me to be able to stand up for myself and thrive. She was, herself, a health professional and a great mentor. She didn't take no for an answer and she didn't take mediocre as acceptable. She was one of my first mentors that taught me if I was to make it happen, it was up to me, to work hard and if it was to be, I had to dare to believe in myself.

Adversity has blessed my path my entire life. I've had to learn to overcome challenges, obstacles, failure and rejection throughout school, my career and in my personal life. I had to learn to lead myself, believe in myself and act boldly and dream big even when others told me, "You're not strong enough, smart enough, or skilled enough." I learned how to overcome adversity time after time. My mother always said that when my sister and I got into trouble (and we did) it was my influence that got us there.

The second adversity that I often refer to relates to me carving out a career in fitness. Although careers in fitness were starting to be shaped during the late 70s, when I was about to graduate, my guidance counselor said that while there were careers for people that have interest in education and fitness, I really needed to look to become a Physical Ed teacher. I love to teach and help others, and teaching would be a great avenue, but I wanted something much bigger and bolder. In my high school yearbook, although I didn't realize it until I looked back on it 2 decades later, I wrote, "Anything to do with fitness, where I can travel the globe, teach and help others, and have a thriving career." My guidance counselor said there was no such career. I ended up going home deflated and sad and I said to my mom, "I want to travel the world, I want to teach others. I'm going to the east coast to teach marine biology," and she said, "Honey, you get seasick on a boat. Why were you thinking about that?" And I said to her, "I was told I couldn't have what I wanted, so that's the next best thing." Somehow, within me, I decided to trust the advice of my guidance counsellor and just go for it. I went into physical health education at Western, as guided by my counselor, but then I soon discovered that there was the opportunity to shape a career and I just went from there.

I'm certain it was my curiosity and natural leadership skills, my passion (or as my mother and teachers would describe as 'high energy'), my "can-do-no-quit" attitude and ability to influence others and most importantly my belief in the cause (more than myself even), where I learned that these character traits would get me through. These are the principles and strengths I possess and I credit to much of my success today.

It seemed like everyone said "No" to me my whole life. And it's that word "No;" as soon as I hear it, my inside voice flips it right away and I say, "No? Watch me." I immediately feel my internal drive switch into gear, my passion come alive and my natural competitive instinct kick in, to prove to myself and others what's possible. "No" is a common word in my life, and I've had to deal with the road blocks that hearing "No" brings along with it throughout my personal life and my career. It just makes me work harder, aim higher, and go faster or further.

As an example, I felt successful the first day I stepped out of university and stepped forward into my career as a group fitness instructor. One day after graduating from my Physical Ed degree, I jumped on a train and walked into the headquarters of a small fitness club chain in Toronto and handed in my one-page resume, in response to the manager job that was posted in the newspaper. I recall fondly being laughed out of the room for my lack of experience, but that didn't hold me back. When asked if I taught aerobics classes, I replied, "Absolutely." Although I had only taught one segment of a fitness class in my four years of university, I was determined to succeed. And with the management willing to have me audition the very next day in my hometown of Oakville, at one of the clubs within that chain, I went home and started putting together a 60-minute dancercise class. I drew inspiration from watching the 20-minute workout TV show, and my household collection of Jane Fonda workout VHS tapes, and I managed to win over the hearts of the class participants and management. Within 3 months, I was teaching 15 primetime classes a week, while working the remainder of the time as a full-time fitness trainer.

While I loved what I was doing in the fitness industry, I returned to Western to attend physiotherapy school. I was passionate about helping others regain their health following injury or illness, and make exercise a part of their lifestyle, as well as their rehabilitation. I also wanted to give back. And as a premature baby with physical challenges early in life and energetic accident-prone kid, I had experienced first-hand the healing powers that physiotherapists possessed, and dreamed about becoming a sport physiotherapist. Little did I know that my struggle to get into (and through) physiotherapy school served a purpose and helped to place me on my unique path.

It was my life mission to improve the lives of people and I live to serve the world by inspiring others, and helping them succeed, by connecting them to people, programs, and services that will assist them in finding their own personal health, wellness, purpose and power.

When the opportunity came to leave what I thought was my dream career to return to the fitness industry, I must have known deep down that there was more instore for me so I took a leap of faith. Of course I was afraid; however, my passion was greater. I left my career as a physiotherapist and, while I maintain my license to practice physiotherapy, I have never looked back.

How I Overcame Adversity, Rejection and Fear

I've committed my life to ongoing learning and personal development. My inspiration for everything comes from watching and following others who are successful—my role models—then striving to achieve the same for myself.

When I am faced with adversity, rejection and fear, I jump in with both feet to address the situation or issue and I seek to find a solution or a path to achievement. I am an over-achiever, goal-oriented and driven woman and I do not like to sit back and allow others to decide my fate or any situation to define or determine my outcome. I have also learned to listen to my '2nd voice' which is my gut instinct. I am still learning every day to listen to my heart, redefine worry into wonder, and get out of my own way.

I have learned to believe in myself, believe in my abilities, believe in the kindness and mentorship of others as well as influence others along my path. While other peoples' judgements and attitudes may momentarily affect me, I am able to change my state (my mindset) and regain my confidence. I've had to learn that over the years, and I've worked with coaches and like-minded leaders to help me regain my strength when I'm going through a tough time.

I exercise daily to keep my mind right, maintain a strong posture and fit body, mind and spirit. I have to give credit to my boss Patch, the CEO and founder of GoodLife Fitness and canfitpro. He has been a great influence in my life. Patch didn't just encourage me to take risks and lead but rather he expected and challenged me to do so. I've been blessed to work alongside very motivating and supportive leaders and I have an abundance of positive, supportive and inspirational mentor and friends as well as a husband who adores me and supports everything I do. I have benefited immensely from having female mentors who are confident to lead in a male dominated industry. They have influenced me to take risks, stretch, grow and believe in myself.

The Importance of a Positive Mindset

Having a positive mindset is everything! Your brain believes everything you tell it. If you believe you can, you can AND you will find a way. If you believe you can't, you're right! You can talk yourself out of everything. I say to members who take my fitness classes that 'the only way you fail is if you quit, never quit!"

5 Tips to Choosing Success Over Adversity:

1. Change your thoughts. Your thoughts create your feelings. Your feelings become words. Your words shape your actions. Your actions shape your behavior. Have a "can-do attitude."

2. Work on building success muscles with exercise. Exercise helps to build resilience, stamina and helps stimulate the neurotransmitters (dopamine) that influence motivation. Other hormones, like testosterone, are key to building motivation (and a sense of power). Exercise also helps you manage stress and the negative effects associated with the adrenal chemical cortisol. Nurture your body—with good nutrition—just as you would nurture your brain (and mindset).

3. Power pose—as a physiotherapist I always focused on posture. Now social psychologists are telling us that posture and power posing is key to improving self-confidence. I practice my three power poses almost

daily and incorporate them into a fitness class I created for GoodLife called NEWBODY.

4. Meditate. I work with a meditation coach to help me with this because my natural high-energy makes it hard for me to sit still and enjoy quiet reflective time. While running is a form of meditation for me, I've realized over the last couple of years the power of a mindful practice and I'm enjoying the clarity and focus it is providing me.

5. Personal development and daily reading and reflection (focusing on gratitude) is key to getting your mind right. While I'm very busy and work long hours, I spend a 15-30 minutes a day focusing on my own personal leadership development. I seek out positive, like-minded people to connect with on a daily basis.

Practicing these strategies daily allows me the opportunity to self-reflect, practice and to learn about myself. I consider these daily rituals to be 'self-care'. Before you can help others and influence the world with your purpose, you must ensure that you are in alignment with your why and in congruency with your passion and purpose.

Over the years, I have learned how to stand up for and believe in myself, to use my voice and share my vision. I've developed these 'super powers' over time and with age comes wisdom. Now in my mid-fifties, I'm more content and clear in who I am and why I exist and this sense of purpose is clearer than ever.

I've got a great story about preparing yourself mentally. Twenty years ago, I was in Australia presenting at a conference. I had injured myself the night before, and I hadn't slept very much because I was in pain. I was supposed to teach a 5-hour workshop starting very early in the morning. I distinctly remember nurturing my body with 1.5 liters of water. I couldn't eat because I didn't feel well.

Before my presentation, I went to the ladies bathroom and I stood in front of the mirror and I said out loud, **"I am confident and I will be the most inspirational, motivating, and knowledgeable leader on this topic; I will go out there and I will make an impact!"** I looked in the mirror, said it out loud, with affirmation, confidence, and boldness. And as I walked out of the bathroom, I noticed that there were two women in the stalls who were probably fearful of walking out, thinking that I thought I was alone and they didn't want to embarrass me for having talked out loud. The best part of all was there was no other workshop that morning, so those two women came to my session! I'll never forget that. I wanted to make a great impression and I did. It was the best presentation, or one of the best, I've ever given in my career.

An important lesson I've learned that still impacts how I live and make decisions today

I have learned to always trust my '2nd voice' which is my gut instinct and use this 'super power' I've been given to speak up and share my vision and my thoughts, no matter if they are incongruent with everyone else. When I do not listen to my 2nd voice, I regret it. Many times, I have learned that my 2nd voice was, in fact, right.

The advice that I would give to others going through a challenging time

Embrace the challenge and welcome the opportunity to learn and grow. Face adversity in the face. Work with a coach to clarify your purpose, your strengths (and 'super power') and your weaknesses (kryptonite).

Understand that adversity is meant to provide you with insight, learning, and the opportunity to become stronger. It will pass, like any storm, and you can only find the 'pot of gold' at the end of the rainbow.

It is easier said than done of course, and I'm continually learning to embrace challenge, like a hard work out. At the end of it all you are stronger and better and have a greater sense of pride and purpose.

Begin with the end in mind. Picture yourself reaching the end of the challenge and reaching success. Visualize, articulate and feel what it will look like, be and feel like when you arrive. Know why you exist. Meditate on this too.

Decide and define your role (how you will serve the world), what your life will be, and what role you will play. Do not play small. You are not here, in this life, to play small. Do not let anyone or anything tell you otherwise.

Be bold, dream big and define your own greatness and own it. This is your life so live it out loud!

About the Author

Maureen (Mo) Hagan

Website: www.mohagan.com
Email: defyaging@golden.net
Phone: 519-870-3070
Facebook: Maureen Hagan
LinkedIn: Maureen Hagan
Instagram: mo_hagan
Twitter: mo_hagan

Mo's work has spanned three decades, with numerous awards for her innovation, passion, instruction and leadership. Mo was inducted into her High school Hall of Fame in 2009, she was named as one of Canada's 20 Most Influential Women in Sport and Physical Activity in 2014, honored with the 2016 IHRSA's "Woman Leader" of the Year and recognized as one of the Optimyz 100 top Health Influencers in Canada (2017).

Mo is a published author and a regular contributor to consumer magazines and on-line publications including the Huffington Post. Mo continues to teach group fitness classes and speaks at health, wellness and fitness conferences around the globe while working full time as a Vice President of Program Innovation at GoodLife Fitness and canfitpro.

Over the years, Mo has set lofty goals for herself and through the guidance and influence of teachers, mentors and coaches and through challenging and rewarding life experiences, Mo ambitiously curated a career in health and fitness, re-shaping health care along the way. It is Mo's life mission to help improve the lives of people and she lives to serve the world by inspiring others and helping them succeed. She accomplishes this through her many roles within the fitness industry as a senior leader for two large Canadian companies, and in her own business as a speaker, coach and visionary.

Chapter 2:

Choosing Love Over Fear to Rise Above Adversity

By Lani Gelera

Lani Gelera is a professional Stuntwoman who has worked on more than 100 movies and TV shows. Also known as The Fenix Fallgirl, she has lived an extraordinary life of worldwide travel, adventure, enterprise, physical challenges and unique opportunities and experiences. She has spent most of her life less ordinary looking for the message that she has to contribute to make a difference in the lives of others. Coming from adversity and beginning her spiritual journey at the early age of 11 has presented many challenges that have gifted her the values of courage, independence and the power of believing in her own self-worth. Lani's current aspirations in life are to share her personal experiences and lessons learned to have a positive influence in others as a role model that inspires self-love, overcoming fears, experiencing life to the fullest and reaching for your highest potential in relationships, career and in contribution to others. She believes that without someone in your life telling you that you should love yourself and you have value, we run the risk of learning this lesson too late in life and not fully reaching our unrealized potential to make a difference in the world.

Falling Down for a Living

Falling down for a living has its ups and downs, no pun intended. There are many things I love about being a stunt woman in TV/Film and there are many physical, mental and emotional challenges that come with this line of work. It's definitely not for everyone. I've always believed that it takes a certain kind of person to face their fears and put themselves out there for the sake of entertainment and earning an income.

I believe we are all unique individuals and I have never been a fan of stereotypes. I know for certain that I do not subscribe to the common preconceived misconceptions of my particular profession. I'm not a daredevil, I am not an adrenaline junkie, I don't have a death wish and I don't take unnecessary or un-calculated risks at work. I do consider myself skilled, courageous, determined, hard working and badass in my own unapologetic way. I also enjoy the fact that I do what I love for a living and I get to challenge myself physically, mentally and live my life to the fullest. There are not many careers where you can experience new things, meet amazing and talented people, challenge yourself in every way, travel and get paid well to do all of it.

I've been a Stuntwoman for 15 years. I am very well aware of the difference between who I really am and who people *think* I am once they learn of my profession. Quite often children and adults alike have assumptions that I'm an extreme athlete and I might break out in a fight or start flipping around at any second. Yes, many performers can be like that, but not all of us. It gets tiresome when people expect me to entertain them or want to know what big names I have worked with or what my scariest stunt was. Although I can always answer these questions to their satisfaction, I often feel very superficial talking about my work in this way. These things truly don't matter to me and I'm not seeking to impress anyone. I honestly feel like I have very little to prove to anyone and that there are more interesting things about me to talk about aside from my career. Like the fact that I believe in magic, my best friends are all unicorns, my favourite number is 22, I've travelled around the world and I have four different ways to fly in my dreams. I love talking about the things that make me different. I can appreciate that my career is fascinating to others that don't work in the industry and I'm happy to answer questions to the best of my experience and knowledge. But there gets to a point where they can start idolizing or fantasizing about my job in a way that sets me so far apart that they just can't relate. I would prefer to talk about the unique aspects of my life that make me just like everyone else and that just about anyone can relate to. Like my fears, my challenges, falling in love, overcoming adversity and the things I'm passionate about in life.

I would much rather talk about the type of person I am and how I became a stuntwoman. I'd much rather connect with people on a more real life, down to earth way. I'm just like everyone else and I have overcome a lot to get to where I am. I'd rather talk about the lessons I've learned and the experiences I have had that have made me who I am today. I truly believe that by sharing my real life story of overcoming adversity, I can possibly inspire and help others to believe in what else is possible in their own lives.

Fallgirl Empowerment Project

I'm very proud of the woman I have become and I believe that everything happens for a reason; every challenge and lesson I have learned in my life has sculpted and molded me through heartache, adventure and adversity. But I have always wondered how much further I could have gone if I had been supported. How much more successful might I have been? How much more powerful might I have become if only I had learned of my own unlimited potential at a younger age?

I often compare my life to those that grew up in a somewhat stable family environment where they were encouraged, supported, and given love and advice. I can see how differently they feel about themselves and see the value of being brought up in an environment where you are taught you have value and you can do anything you really want to with hard work and perseverance. I can see the advantage of these influences in comparison to the lack of family dynamics, support and love that I experienced.

It's taken me a good 30 years to learn how to love and value myself and start to believe in myself the way I have always wanted others to. I believe that young women of today can benefit greatly from learning these lessons of overcoming fear, believing in yourself and the power of your dreams, early on. If only they had the right influences around them, they could literally change the world. Through my experiences and professional career, I seek to empower young women and give them the tools, lessons and skills needed to move forward in their own lives, realize their true potential and accomplish their dreams.

With this in mind, I have designed a workshop along with other stuntwomen for girls in the foster care system age 14 to 19. I want to be that person who says to them, "You have value, you have worth and you have unlimited potential."

In the workshops, we do all sorts of activities on overcoming fears, physical challenges, finding balance in life, believing in yourself, and the effectiveness of journaling and writing down your thoughts. That's so therapeutic and so powerful. I want to give them these tools to empower them moving forward in their lives.

Everyone has a story to tell about their own unique lives that will contribute to the growth and empowerment of others in some way along their journey. I did not have enough of those kind of powerful female influences and representatives in my life to look up to when I was growing up. I want to be able to share these tools I have learned and invest in these young women and our collective future.

What Inspired Me to Want to Empower Young Women?

I've been looking for a way to contribute to my community for many years using my personal experiences and lessons learned. I started developing my empowerment program for girls in foster care in the summer of 2016 after learning some pretty big lessons through heartache and heartbreak. Like every other relationship in my life, I left this one feeling rejected and completely abandoned by someone I had given my heart and soul to. I didn't realize it at the time, but it was the same old lesson I was meant to learn my whole life. The pain of loss and loneliness, crying myself to sleep and wondering why this was all happening to me, once again, was so great after a couple of months that finally, I started to get it. I started to realize just how low my own self-worth was and how my breakup was a reflection of how I actually felt about myself. I started to realize that my whole life I had very low self-worth and it was prevalent in every area of my life: My family, relationships, career and how I showed up in the world and contributed to others.

It wasn't until that summer that I recognized that my life long low self-worth was a result of the rejection and abandonment from my father at the age of 11.

I set out to start building my own self love and discover my own value and worth. Through life coaching, counselling, energy healing, meditation, lots of time in nature, exercise, a couple great books and many glasses of wine with friends, I slowly started recovering my power and healing myself.

One of the most powerful things I did to heal my fear of rejection and abandonment was the call I made to my father to tell him I was coming over to talk. I went to visit my dad, 2 months after my breakup, and I told him what was happening in my life. I had never really talked to my dad before. My mother mostly raised my sister and I when she was alive. Since then I had seen my dad maybe 3-4 times a year on holidays and birthdays. So I began to tell him that I was depressed, I had a breakup with my boyfriend, I closed down one of my businesses and I was feeling that I had very low self-worth. Then I told him where I felt my low self-worth came from and I asked him the questions that I had waited 30 years to ask, "Why did you give me away when I was 13? Why did you not see any value in me as a daughter?"

He didn't have any answers but I could see he was getting upset and remorseful so then I asked him, "What were your family dynamics like? How were your parents with you growing up?"

He went on to explain that he came from a very large family of 11 and he was the second to youngest. Daily life was all about raising livestock, growing food, fishing and going to school. His biggest dreams were to move to Canada and be successful. Basically he described a family environment very different from how I had been raised but I came to realize that maybe my father wasn't capable of being a loving, supportive, encouraging father to me because he didn't have those tools. Maybe he wasn't raised that way himself. Maybe my father just did the best he could with the tools that he had at the time and giving me away was what he thought was best for me.

In that conversation I found compassion for my father and I began to realize that giving me away had nothing to do with my value or worth as a daughter and that it had everything to do with where and who he was at the time. It was a reflection of him, not me. That conversation was the ultimate healing and went a long way for me in overcoming my fears of rejection, abandonment and low self-worth. Before you heal these things you must acknowledge them and call them by their name - FEAR. Then you must go back to their origin and process the trauma that caused them from your current state of consciousness. With your current wiser, more mature awareness, you can choose to see the situation with love and compassion so that you can finally and ultimately heal that wounded child within.

Some pretty big life lessons were learned last summer. And it's because I have taken so much away from these life lessons of self-love, confidence and worthiness, that I want to share these lessons with others in a way that can make a real difference. I want these teen foster girls to know their worth, to have someone to look up to, to have some positive examples of what they can achieve when they believe in themselves.

Becoming a Stunt Woman

Growing up in the Lower Mainland of British Columbia, I never realized that being a Stuntwoman was a career option for me until I was 27 years old. I have a background in gymnastics and during my school years I was involved in every sport and activity that my teenage schedule would allow. I was into all physical endeavours and enjoyed challenging myself and improving my skills.

I went to college for Computer Programming and got a job as a Systems Integration Analyst when I graduated. After a year I chose to become a Fitness Instructor because it better suited my sense of adventure, personality and physical aptitude. Almost immediately I obtained a job as a Fitness Instructor on cruise ships and ended up travelling around the world for 3 years teaching hi-lo and step classes at sea. After 9/11 I felt compelled to come home and get a "real job" although I had no idea what that meant for me.

In the fall of 2001, while dropping in at adult gymnastics at a local gym one evening, I was bouncing on my own on the trampoline when I saw two women fighting across the gym. I stopped and watched them for a while only to realize that their fight was choreographed. I couldn't resist asking them what they were doing. They said that they were stuntwomen and they were putting together a fight scene for a show. That was the first time that I found out you could be a stuntman in Vancouver. I was so intrigued and asked them where I could go train with other stuntpeople. They directed me to Cameron Rec. Centre in Coquitlam on Thursday nights adult drop-in. I went and my stunt career started right there with the training, networking, promotion and putting myself out there.

With a lot of dedication, focus and direction, I was in the Union of BC Performers by the end of 2002. Meeting those two stuntwomen changed everything for me. They came along in perfect timing, right when I was asking the Universe how I could be self-employed, doing what I love, making a living and using my life long acquired skills and talents. It was one of many examples of perfect synchronicity in my life.

How Teenage Drama Becomes Lifelong Trauma

I had a great deal of sadness and adversity after my mother passed away. When I was 11 years old, we were on a family camping trip in the middle of my uncle's farm in a pasture, like we did every summer. My mom had been suffering from nausea and vomiting for a while. She went to the bathroom and she just started vomiting and while she was vomiting, a blood vessel burst and she collapsed. I remember that my sister tried to resuscitate her, but it was too late. We were out in the middle of a farm and it was more than an hour-and-a-half before an ambulance came out. There was nothing they could do.

My dad wasn't there. It was only me and my sister, and my grandma and my grandpa. And it was my grandma's birthday.

My life changed in an instant. I was so close to my mom and now she was gone. My dad was working a lot, and not active as a parent. He didn't have a clue how to raise 2 teenage daughters on his own so he prioritized finding a new wife above all else. A year later, he got married to a 27-year-old Filipino woman, which was a completely different culture than my mother's. My mother was French Canadian.

His new wife was very demanding of me and I remember she had these lists of chores we had to do. She was not loving. I remember getting into fights with her sometimes and I would say, "You're not my mother! You can't tell me what to do!" and she would say things like, "Of course I'm not your mother - your mother's dead!" She was really not compassionate. What I needed was for her to love me, and hug me, and tell me that everything was going to be ok. I was grieving.

And the truth is I was a teenager. I was going through a really difficult time that I didn't know how to process. I was rebellious. In reality, I was on the honour roll in school, I was in every sport and activity, I was a good kid.

My Stepmom and I didn't get along and a lot of our fights turned physical. Instead of trying to manage that or figure that out, my father just kicked me out of the house when I was 13-years-old. I remember how he threw all my belongings in garbage bags and kicked me out of the house.

To add to that, he legally gave custody of me away to the courts so that he would not have to pay for my living expenses. He wanted to start his family over. To me it was the ultimate rejection and abandonment from my only parent left and it told me that he saw no value in me as a daughter. I believed that I wasn't worth keeping in his life, so he just gave me away.

Technically I was in the foster care system, meaning I was a ward of the court. But I was only actually in a foster home for a couple of months and then I moved in with my friends. I didn't like living with a stranger like that. So I moved in with my friends until I was 16 and then I moved in with my boyfriend. Then I moved out on my own when I was 18.

The government paid for my living expenses up until I was 18 and they gave me a grant for college, which I used to go to Douglas College to get a Diploma in Computer Information Systems.

Learning to Listen to My Own Inner Guidance

I never felt supported as a teen or young adult. I didn't feel like I could rely on anyone, and that was prevalent in every area of my life. For a time after I graduated I did things I thought I was supposed to, not because I truly wanted to. The reason I became a computer programmer was because I thought that would make my father proud. I suppose I was still trying to win his love, but he wasn't impressed at all. I did it for a year and hated it. I lost the desire to do anything for someone else, because I was supposed to or to make others happy. I eventually quit my job as a Systems Integration Analyst after a year and started to listen to my inner voice within. That voice told me to start doing things I enjoyed and made me feel good, so as I mentioned, I became a Fitness Instructor and traveled the world for three years, teaching on a cruise ship.

I started to follow my own heart and intuition. I didn't rely on people at all and along with that, I wasn't open to taking advice from people. I'm sure it was well meant, but I didn't feel that anybody knew my situation and my circumstances, nor had any right to tell me what they thought I should be doing.

Sure, I've made a lot of mistakes along my way in life. But I've learned a great deal of important life lessons from those mistakes. And if I didn't learn the lesson, it was sure to show up again and again until I did.

Being a teen on my own with no parents to guide me was not ideal. The relationship that I was in when I was 16 was not healthy by any means. I had no one in my life that told me that I didn't have to settle for the first guy that paid attention to me. It was very emotionally and physically abusive and there were a lot of drugs and crime. My boyfriend at that time was a total nightmare and I was with him for 6 years. I tried to leave him after 4 years and he wouldn't let me leave him. It was a toxic and unhealthy relationship that I accepted simply because I wanted to be feel wanted, needed and worthy. It was a big lesson in self-worth that I didn't even learn till much later in life.

I didn't have any parental influence at that time. If a friend's parents tried to give me advice, I just didn't think they had the right to. Because of this, I learned to listen to my inner guidance and intuition early on in life. I started doing things that just felt right and I started believing that I was being guided and that maybe things are not happening to me, but for me to learn.

Remembering My Mom

My childhood memories were very loving and full of family get togethers, activities, outdoor adventures and camping. My mother was a very influential and positive part of my life, always encouraging my creativity, sense of adventure and love of the outdoors and natural environment. She was very active in all areas of my life as my softball coach, my girl guides and brownies leader, the hot dog lady at school and always encouraging hikes and camping outdoors. My mother ran a daycare from home and was always present, always there in my life until the day she passed away.

Not long after she passed away I remember having a dream of my mother standing in front of me, trying to be there for me. I've had very lucid dreams my entire life and when I dreamt of my mother standing in front of me it felt so real it scared me because I was fully aware that she had just passed. I began to cry uncontrollably, in my dream, at the sight of my mother. She told me that she would not come back to me until I could handle her presence, and I didn't dream of her again for more than a decade.

I always had a sense of adventure from my mother so a lot of those things were strengthened and further developed in my teenage years. My spiritual journey began the day she passed, and I started asking questions about, "Where did she go?" "What happens when we die?" In my 20s, my connection with my mother was regained when I was strong enough and unafraid to handle her presence.

I always knew that she was around, but it was confirmed when I was working on cruise ships and I had a Reiki treatment. It was my very first one and I was unfamiliar with the Reiki practitioner. I lay down on the table, and 5 minutes later, the first thing he said was, "Is your mother still alive?" And I said, "No, she passed away. Why?" And he said, "She's in the room. She's always been there, whenever you need her."

That was my confirmation because I always felt her there. And ever since, every time I've had my heart broken, I've jumped off buildings, or gotten into car crashes for my job, she helped me overcome the fear, and gave me the strength and reassurance that I'm never truly alone. I'm never alone. She is always watching over me.

My Love For Travel

I've done a lot of travelling on my own and every one of my adventures or trips that I've been on has been a soul searching kind of experience. If I'm not in a relationship, I always tend to run away from the holidays. I don't like to be at home for Christmas. Christmas is all about family and I kind of just go out into the world and I try and find myself at that time.

One year I went to Cuba for 6 weeks on my own over the holidays. I rented a little apartment on the seaside of Miramar, outside Havana, and learned Spanish and practiced guitar. The following year I travelled to Peru on my own and hiked the Inca Trail to Machu Picchu, visited Lake Titicaca, Ollantaytambo, Cusco and stayed in the Amazon Jungle.

I recently drove down to Mexico by myself in 4 days and I didn't know anybody when I got there. I stayed for almost a month, met so many amazing people and learned how to

Kiteboard, living on the beach. The people that have come into my space are supportive, caring, inspiring and drawn to my energy as well. It's all so perfectly synchronistic. I've learned to ask for what I want in my life and trust that the universe has my back and all that I want will show up through circumstance and the people I meet.

My stunt work mostly takes place in Vancouver (Hollywood North), but every once in a while, I end up travelling across the country, like Toronto or Alberta, or across British Columbia to work on various productions that request me.

The Importance of a Strong Mindset

I believe that how you feel about yourself and how you perceive your environment has everything to do with the influences and role models you have had in your life. Importantly, I think that the very first relationships that you have in life set the tone for all of the other relationships that you have moving forward.

My relationship with my mom was one of love, support and kindness. But after she died and my dad gave me away, I began to believe that I was worthless. I thought I was not worthy of love. In my child's mind, my dad gave me away because he didn't want me and I was unlovable.

Nobody ever told me that I'm supposed to love myself. How was I supposed to know that when there was nobody in my life to show me that I'm supposed to love and believe in myself, and that I had unlimited potential?

My mindset in my younger years was one of low self-worth and wanting to prove myself and being very independent, and figuring things out on my own. That's the whole reason I started my project working with teen girls. I want to provide that powerful influence and role model, just for those girls. I want to be the one that says, "You are powerful beyond measure. You can do this." I want to be the positive influence that was lacking for me.

Do you know the story of the 4-minute mile? Before Roger Bannister ran a mile in under 4 minutes, no one thought it was possible. Everyone said it was physically impossible to run a mile in under 4 minutes. People tried, and they all failed, because they all believed that it was not possible. When Roger Bannister broke the record in 1954, the limiting belief that it was impossible was shattered, and soon after, others began to be able to do it. Since 1954, more than 1,000 men have run the mile in under 4 minutes.

That's the power of a role model or an influence. I want to be able to tell girls how valuable they are and how special they are. I want to be an influence, and something for them to look up to and aspire to.

I overcame my low self-worth in my 30's by finally recognizing it and actively seeking inspiration, guidance and encouragement to develop myself love and confidence. It's taken me more than 30 years to learn how to love myself and how doing so affects every area of my life.

I have developed a strong sense of independence, courage and spirituality and connection to my mother's spirit that has guided me my entire life.

I have always sought adventure, physical sports and activities, yoga meditation and a deep and meaningful connection with others to draw my strength from and move forward in life.

Mindset Matters

All of life is but a classroom and every single person that comes into your life is nothing more than an assignment, a lesson to learn about living and love.

Overcoming adversity is nothing more than learning the lessons that are presented to you and working towards healing your wounded heart and soul so that you can move forward in your life powerfully with love.

Mindset is everything. First you must be aware of your thoughts and how they reflect how you feel about yourself. Then you must consciously choose empowering and positive thoughts that will help you process the adversity or challenges that you have faced so that you can learn the lesson and move forward in your life without holding onto any negativity or resentment. Overcoming adversity is a universal assignment that you have been given to grow you into the person that you are meant to become and your mindset will determine how you approach this assignment and how many times you will be presented with it.

One of my favourite books I have recently read on keeping a positive mindset in life is called *The Universe Has Your Back* by Gabrielle Bernstein. This powerful book inspires the reader to turn all of their fears into faith and believe that everything happens for a reason and we are constantly being guided towards love, our greater good and ultimate desires.

6 Tips to Choosing Success

1. Learn to love yourself and acknowledge your own self-worth and unlimited power and potential. Your success in life is direct reflection of how you value and love yourself. You have to love yourself first, above everything and everyone else in order to show up in the world with the confidence, power and grace you will need to be successful in any area. When you truly get this and start taking care of yourself, believing in yourself and loving yourself then your life will start shifting and moving in all the necessary ways toward success.

2. Take care of yourself - body, mind and soul. Educate yourself on healthy foods and be conscious of what you are putting into your body and how it affects your energy, your moods, your attitude and your perception of the world around you. Food is an important part of the equation in how you feel about yourself and how successful you will be. Physical exercise is important to keep the flow of energy moving throughout your body. Challenge yourself through physical sports and activities. Meditation is one of the most powerful tools or methods of aligning your energy with the universal flow and working towards manifesting your goals and desires. Take a meditation course, learn some techniques and try to incorporate some form of meditation into your life to elevate your personal

energetic vibration and draw more positivity into your life.

3. Find things you are passionate about that light your soul on fire. Spend most of your time doing activities you love. Develop a career that you love and are proud of. Find a creative outlet that lets you share your love and passion with others. When you spend the majority of your time feeling good about yourself, what you are doing and how you are earning your living, more of that positive energy (and money) will be drawn into your life. "Do what you love and the money will come."

4. Face your fears, whatever they are. Acknowledge all the fears you have in your life and how they are holding you back. Call out your fear and choose love instead. Do something that scares you every day. There is a lesson for you in the process of overcoming those things that hold you back whether they are emotional or physical. Face them, learn from them and realize your own powerful unlimited potential.

5. Develop self confidence in all areas of your life. Start by learning about the things that interest you. Become good at the things you love to do! Take care of yourself and your appearance. When you build your self confidence in all areas you also build your personal vibration and attract more of the positive things you want in your life and other people that will help you accomplish your goals.

6. Be Open to Guidance when it comes into your life. It might be in the form of friendly advice, a book you feel inspired to read or a movie you recently saw. Be

conscious of your inner voice and the language you are using. Your words are powerful – keep them positive. Ask for guidance from your higher self, the universe, your spirit guides. Ask for help and pay attention to the signs when they come. Believe in your own ability to overcome adversity.

Overcoming Adversity: Becoming Your Best Self

Maybe overcoming adversity is all about becoming the best version of yourself possible. Maybe in order for you to discover how strong, powerful, capable and incredible you really are, you need to be challenged in the most difficult and painful ways in life. Maybe without those challenges you would never realize your own self-worth and unlimited potential.

I'm a big believer that everything happens for a reason in our lives. We don't often know what those reasons are until we look back from a distance and it all makes sense. It makes sense because, given some time and viewed from afar, we can put the pieces of the puzzle together and see that we have become who we are because of our experiences in life. And when and if we come to a place where we can appreciate and start loving ourselves for who we are, we have to then also appreciate the fact that our past experiences have forged us through heartache, heartbreak, challenges, lessons and loss. When we learn to love ourselves, we learn to see our lives as a huge universal lesson and every experience is an assignment.

We are never faced with an assignment we can't handle, but if we refuse to learn the lesson, the assignment will keep showing up in our lives over and over again. Once we have done the self work, learned the lesson and grown because of it, we are then presented with another, different lesson. And so our lives go on, lesson after lesson. Each one molding us and creating our own unique perspective of the world.

Overcoming adversity is all about learning the life lessons and using them to move forward in life, not staying stuck in the same old lesson. Your lessons are your own. No one can learn them for you. You will be surrounded by those that will give you advice, support, encouragement and lots of information. There will also be plenty of people around you that will criticize, judge or condemn you. You have to decide for yourself what you want to believe and what resonates with you. You have to discover your own intuitive power and your own ability to choose the life you want to live.

Overcoming adversity is about discovering your independence, your inner strength, courage, personal power and ability to handle any challenge that crosses your life path.

I believe that the more adversity you have overcome in life, the more experience you have to share with others, the more compassion you develop for others and the more confidence you develop within yourself.

No matter what has happened in your life or how you have been hurt, abused, rejected, abandoned or tortured.... there was something for you to learn from your experience and something that you can take from it to make you stronger, wiser and more loving.

There are many ways to heal yourself and your life. I highly recommend a book called *You Can Heal Your Life* by Louise Hay. This will introduce you to the concept of your energetic body and how it is a reflection of your life. Everything is connected.

You will be guided to the right teacher, coach, counsellor, healer or inspiration in perfect timing and when you are ready and open to receive it.

About the Author

Lani Gelera

Website: www.fenixfallgirl.com
Facebook:
www.facebook.com/Fenixfallgirl
Email: lanigelera@hotmail.com

Lani is a Professional Stunt-woman who has been working in Film/Tv for the past 15 years, living in Squamish, BC. She has a passion for travel, adventure, many activities and following her dreams. Always learning in life and striving to help family and friends while contributing to her community.

Chapter 3:

Running the Race of Life

By Mariam Griffith

Mariam Griffith migrated to America by herself with a one way ticket to fulfill her dreams. She has built a phenomenal business in Real Estate as a multi-million dollar producer and has become a very successful Real Estate investor. She has grown as a leader throughout the Industry. A truly self-made professional, now she focuses on empowering others to unlock their unlimited beliefs so that they can fulfill their true purpose. She is a published co-author of a best-selling book, How to Buy & Sell Real Estate in Today's Market.

This is her inspiring story of how she faced adversities and became a successful professional. She tells of her remarkable journey with great passion and enthusiasm.

A Martial-Law Baby

I was born in Lucena City in Quezon, a province on the southern coast of Luzon Island, Philippines. My mother was a schoolteacher. She was a widow who struggled to raise me and my two brothers in one of the most typhoon-battered areas of the country.

Every year, an average of more than a dozen tropical cyclones visit the Philippine archipelago during the months of August to November, most of them ironically churned and driven from the Pacific Ocean. Being essentially an agricultural nation, many Filipinos derive their means of livelihood from farming, fishing and small mining operations – jobs that practically stand still during the stormy months. And many farmers and ordinary business concerns lose millions yearly due to floods and strong winds wrought by the ubiquitous typhoons. Personally, I can say that every Filipino encounters more than his/her fair share of natural disasters in a lifetime.

And we are only talking of natural calamities! The ones caused by man can be equally devastating. You see, I grew up during the Martial Law years under President Ferdinand Marcos, which defined my personal view of how governance in my beloved homeland had failed to provide the relief and progress the people badly needed. For many years until now, my crestfallen country has remained an economically depressed nation for many other reasons I cannot mention. Under such dire circumstances, I grew up seeing considerable adversities as well as poverty all around me.

One story that launched my inevitable journey through adversity and opportunity happened when I was only four years old. Every day, a man with a homemade pushcart walked by our home buying used bottles and old newspapers to sell at the nearby junk shop. I had often wondered what he did with the useless things he collected until my mother told me that it was his livelihood. That moment of realization brought deep compassion inside me every time I saw the man making his rounds. I felt compelled to do something to help him. So, one day I decided to break open my piggy bank and give all my savings to him. My mother was not very happy at what I did, even though she appreciated my deed of kindness.

At such an early stage in my life, I realized I had the capacity to empathize with people who were undergoing adversity. Yes, my family and I were just a few of the numerous Filipinos who had to grind our teeth through the gloomy years of economic and political crises that beset our country then. But for me, it was only the inauspicious beginning of my growing awareness of my role in the infinitely encompassing arena of life.

The Eyes Are the Windows of Our Souls

At the thrilling threshold of entering college, I had the sudden compulsion to join a photography contest for a government-sponsored social-awareness campaign. It was my sure ticket to college, if I won the grand prize. But I had never been a photographer before that; and I did not even own a camera! Yet, I found a way to borrow one and decided to secure the assistance of my old friend, the junk vendor, as my portrait model. He agreed to pose for the photo session; so I took him to a farm nearby where I had him wear some props as I merrily clicked away. With youthful spunk, I entitled my piece as "Needless to Say".

Call it beginner's luck; but my photo won first prize! My dream of going to college had become a reality at that moment of triumph. I had my ticket to a highly-coveted education for many of the youth in my small rural town. But no matter how eager I was to step into college, my mind kept going back to my friend who really gave me the prize. In my simple way of looking at things, I came to the conclusion that he needed and deserved the money more than I did. Although I had envisioned and taken the photograph, it was he who gave life to his own story and the real struggles that he was going through.

Needless to say, he was more than a photography model; he was a living truth. My eyes – still to this day – are mere windows to the adversities I see around me. So, on I went to visit him at his place in the slums and gave him the entire prize money. I did not stay for long since I was not familiar with the place and felt a bit wary. Still, I had time to thank my new found friend for having helped me get the prize and he showed his own gratitude through his copious tears.

I did go to college through a scholarship and finished with a degree in Political Science. Education opens up our minds and our world to other possibilities. The exhilarating adventures of life jump out of books and great challenges and opportunities flow out of lofty ideals taught in the academe. The town I lived in slowly became a tiny village compared to the sprawling metropolitan areas dotted with rising skyscrapers and long bridges spanning great rivers and bays. I gradually became one of thousands of Filipinos who aspired to leave the country and find a new life abroad, if not a new job, at least. The '70's to the '80's ushered in the great Filipino diaspora, filling up jobs at all levels in the Middle East, Asia, Europe and the US. Every working day, a long line of visa applicants formed at the US Embassy in Manila. It would become my own dream to migrate one day.

Big City Blues

After graduating from college, I worked with the Philippine Information Agency, which was a government agency under the Office of the President of the Philippines who was then President Cory Aquino, the reluctant would-be president and widow of the late Senator Benigno Aquino, the nemesis of Marcos. Under her administration, the nation – newly revived by the peaceful EDSA Revolution which toppled Marcos -- would undergo intense economic, political, military and natural crises. It was battered by several coup d'état attempts which brought widespread turmoil and setting back whatever meager advances had been achieved during the 14 years of Martial Law.

My heart truly went out to my fellow Filipinos during those post-Marcos years. In 1990, a Magnitude 7.7 earthquake violently shook two major cities in Northern Luzon, killing hundreds of people inside collapsed buildings. The following year, Mt. Pinatubo erupted after more than five hundred years of dormancy, spewing billions of tons of pyroclastic materials and burying towns and also killing hundreds caught in the natural cataclysm. But such adversities were merely the *coup de grace* divinely appointed for a people who had to suffer the consequences of poor governance.

Since I worked in Manila, the primary business district of the country, I had an interesting and stable job. The small-town lass had become a big-city working woman. It also allowed me to see firsthand what was happening to the nation at large, something that was close to my heart as a Political Science graduate. Then, one of the most violent coups took place right at the heart of Makati. It was both scary and overwhelming to be in the middle of a violent stand-off between government forces and rebels in the military. The imminent danger and the continuing national crisis forced me to take stock of my life and to plan for my family's future. My desire to go abroad became even more compelling so I could move my family to a place where we could be free from the unending chaos around us.

I knew I was not alone with such thoughts. Somewhere out there, I knew I could also make a better life for me and my family.

Crossing the Pacific Ocean

I find myself wondering why California -- and San Francisco, in particular, which was my new place of residence -- does not have the yearly cyclones that plague Asia even though it is right beside the Pacific Ocean. Yes, we do have earthquakes and may someday find ourselves under the Pacific, as they say. But this is now home for me; and as life goes on, adversities are not far behind, as we all know.

I had migrated to the US in 1992 by myself with the intent on achieving success after having gone through so many struggles in my childhood. All those years, I've been striving to maintain the passion and to develop my skills in order to achieve my dreams. I landed a job in the dot-com industry in San Francisco, one of the birthplaces of several IT giants. The industry was then an emerging challenger to the traditional manufacturing and investment enterprises. Being a fresh migrant in the US, I found it a wide open field of opportunity for a young and eager adventurer out to prove her worth. My education and experiences gave me enough confidence to contribute my share in the growing world of enterprise and innovation in one of the most progressive states in the US.

Somehow, I felt I belonged in the cosmopolitan environment I found myself in. Although I did not have formal training in programming or computer languages, I worked myself up the ranks and became a senior analyst at Nextcard, Inc. We were the pioneer of introducing the virtual credit card. At night, I attended classes in IT and soon learned the ropes in the highly-profitable bubble that no one knew was about to burst.

All the while, living in San Francisco showed me the great potential that the United States could offer to anyone who had the heart and mind to ride the economic boom during those years. I had always admired people who practiced civil engineering, particularly my uncle who inspired me with his intellectually challenging and lucrative profession. The process of building an impressive structure on vacant land fascinated me immensely. Whereas I had majored in a college degree that dealt mainly with ideas and abstract principles, I cherished the opportunity to get my hands literally on tangible and visible works of human ingenuity. And seeing all the tall and imposing skyscrapers in the large US cities led me to consider real estate as an alternative occupation.

So, I made the decision to leave the dot-com industry to try my hand at being a Realtor in San Francisco. Most, if not all, of my friends and colleagues thought I was out of my mind to leave at such a time when dot-com was riding high. But my mind was set and I left to pursue a new career.

The Bubble Bursts, the Towers Crumble

In less than a year, the dot-com industry lost steam and crashed in 2000. How happy and grateful I felt for having left at the right moment. Just like in my younger days, I knew I had a guardian angel who was there by my side showing me the way and helping me make decisions that proved to be beneficial for myself and my family even if I did not fully understand the circumstances or the possible consequences then. As the Bible puts it, All things work out for good to those who are called according to God's purpose.

If I thought I had seen the last of adversity's grim face when I left the Philippines, I would have been self-deceived. For certain, adversity follows us wherever we go in this world. Two memorable experiences prove that my newfound country has its own share of struggles and misfortunes. And I was caught, thankfully indirectly, in the midst of two such world-shattering events.

The first one was right after the 9/11 disaster in New York. I was scheduled to fly out three days after 9/11 from San Francisco to Canada. Until that time, airports and airlines were on red alert status. Every plane in the air was a potential bomb, as far as FAA was concerned. It was not the best time to fly; but we were scheduled to fly and we did so in spite of the ominous circumstances.

During that flight, instead of feeling as nervous as the rest of the passengers, I found myself acting more as a coach rather than being coached. It dawned on me that we could either become fearful and fall victim to the terrorist's primary end (to instill fear) or we could be victors and resolve to stand by the promises of the Almighty (*Do not fear!*). So, I decided to gently converse with some of the passengers and make them feel at ease. I consider nervousness a result of the body dissipating wasted energy and calmness a result of the spirit controlling that energy. What could have been a horrifying experience for many helped me to discover an inner strength to know and to harness the power to face adversity.

The whole nation was on its knees at the moment that the twin towers crumbled into dust. But in an instant, people realized we had to stand up, pick up the pieces and rebuild our lives. **Adversity is the best university in life. It teaches us to reach out and find what we are truly capable of.**

When Spectators Become Suspects

The second event occurred during the Boston Marathon in 2013.

I am a marathon runner, having participated in the San Francisco marathon in 1998. Of course, the primary goal of every marathon runner is to run in Boston. It was on a trip to Boston, not to run but merely to observe and feel the excitement, that the next lesson in adversity came. And it was far beyond exciting!

The euphoria of being in Boston to watch the marathon was close to being on Mt. Olympus itself. Even as an observer, the palpable throbbing of one's heart mimics the pumping heart of a marathoner while running the whole 26 miles. My daydream of vicariously running the Boston marathon was broken by a bomb exploding in the midst of the spectators. Euphoria turned into bedlam. Cheers into chaos. Joy into grief. Though unhurt but shaken, I was right at the center of the darkness and madness that followed.

For the next several hours, my friends and I were confined in a car. Ironically, running was no longer an option. We had become suspects as well, not just mere spectators. Cellphone signals were cut off. The police told us not to budge. They banged on our windows to interrogate us.

Again, during the time we were huddled inside the car, I found myself having to act as coach and encourager to my friends. I did not feel we were in real danger, only unwilling extras in a movie where the stars shot each other for real. Yes, we were practically within a battle zone; but we were neither the perpetrators nor the direct victims. **We had a choice to be beneficiaries of whatever lesson the whole thing had in store for us.** My old formula for facing adversity came into good use once more. **We can be victors, not victims!**

Living With a Purpose

I cannot explain or justify why I act or behave the way I do. As a child, I did things that I thought were right the way I saw them. Others may not have accepted my own terms; yet I saw to it that I did what I had decided to do. In that, there is no regret, only a glad realization that things worked out well for me and, in most cases, I was vindicated in my decisions.

As adults, we all think we make our own decisions for ourselves. Nevertheless, there are moments when we have no choice but to act according to what others or what a greater force compels us to do. **We can either submit or rebel.**

We have a choice. But to act so that we always work for and in the truth requires great courage. This is what keeps me going and doing the things I do in my life.

As a virtual runner, I pace myself among the hundreds of other runners. I remind myself of where I came from (the starting line), where I am now (running the race) and what I hope to attain (the prize). The challenges may vary; but the process of preparing for any one of them remains the same. My formula for facing life's adversities, whether my own or those of others, has been a gift I received from an inexplicable source since I was a child. Yet, my short journey through life has already taught me to apply that essential principle in ways that allow me to rise above the mass of humanity running the same race in life.

I am victor, not a victim. And as one, I do not run alone. I seek out those who are victims of misfortunes, so they may continue in their race with courage and dignity.

Like all believers, I have a noble purpose whose reward is worth much more than a gold medal – Abundant Eternal Life. As Apostle Paul put it: "I press on toward the goal for the prize of the upward call of God in Christ Jesus." (Phil. 3:14 NASB)

5 Tips on How to Succeed

I leave the reader with five tips on how to succeed in spite of all the adversities we face on the road to our destiny.

1. Believe in something greater than yourself or your abilities. Are you an accomplished musician or a

smart student? What you have comes from a deeper and greater source which is inexhaustible.

2. Find the purpose of life first before you can start living with purpose. Each day you live with that purpose in mind is a successful day.

3. Adversity never lasts. Winter gives way to spring. The night's darkness to the morning light. It teaches us to persevere, to wait and to overcome our weaknesses.

4. Every trial we overcome, no matter how small, is a step toward maturity. We do not grow old. We only gain what we need to know about how life becomes abundant even when others think we are running out of it.

5. Death is not the worst adversity we can ever face. It is the lack of willingness to see the truth that those who believe in God will never die. Unbelief, although seen as a mere choice, is the very death of the soul.

About the Author

Mariam Griffith

Keller Williams Realty
Brentwood, CA
Phone : 925-759-4538
Email: mariamsells@sbcglobal.net

Born in the Philippines and migrated to the US in 1992, Mariam Griffith is a pure example of the saying that the only thing we need to make our dreams become reality is the simple decision to place success over adversity. Although she was born in a third world country, her upbringing implanted morals and ethics in her personality. Since her childhood, she has been educated to feel the pain of less privileged people. She has spent most of her childhood with her mother and grandmother who respect humanity above everything. It is their firm belief to serve God by showing love and affection to their fellow men. She has always believed in building and developing other people rather than pushing them into the pits of despondencies.

Mariam has a degree in Political Science and worked at the Office of the President in the Philippines during the Presidency of Corazon Aquino. She is the first generation in her family to migrate to the US. During this time period, she determines her future goals and ambitions and focuses on growth personally, socially, economically and spiritually. She enriches herself by sitting in the company of individuals who have a positive attitude towards life.

Mariam is a licensed Real Estate Agent and has been practicing in the San Francisco Bay Area since 1999. She is committed to providing her clients with the most current and up-to-date market information. She dedicates herself to a constant regiment of local economy research.

Her life and ambitions are not just limited to her career and profession of the real estate business. She loves and respects humanity so she always tries to inspire hope, courage, optimism and confidence among others and to be a source of comfort and motivation to others by empowering them with something that improves and changes their lives.

Chapter 4:

Overcoming Adversity
Think Yourself™ Over It!

Nathalie Plamondon-Thomas

Nathalie Plamondon-Thomas is one of the most inspiring and positive people on the planet. She truly walks her talk. She is a Life coach and master NLP practitioner, certified personal trainer and instructor with over 28 years of experience in the fitness industry. She is also a nutrition and wellness specialist and weight loss expert. Nathalie is incredible at helping people achieve their personal, professional, and health & fitness goals.

Nathalie empowers her clients to find within themselves what they need to be their best selves, stay focused and reach their goals all while feeling great. She doesn't give advice. She helps them recreate new neuro-pathways inside their brains which changes their internal dialogue and creates long-term positive transformational changes.

About My Business

My business is called DNA Life Coaching. I am a life coach, a speaker, and a best-selling author. With my coaching and speaking, the message is always, "You have everything you need inside of you," and I teach people a way to access it.

Our brain is the most powerful structure in the universe. It can do everything. Asleep or awake, it controls every moment of your life and it controls everything you do. Unfortunately, for a lot of people, they use their thinking time and their brain in order to make their life worse. They worry with their thinking time, they worry about stuff that won't even happen, they worry about stuff that has already happened. It is done and they choose to re-live it over and over in their head, or they worry about nonsense, like, "What kind of shoes am I going to wear?" or "It's snowing and I don't have anything to remove the snow from my windshield!" Those are the type of worries that we have.

Only about 8% of all of our worries are really worthwhile. We should be using 8% of our thinking time to worry about that stuff but the rest is not necessary. I teach people how to use that 92% of the time that they think, to reprogram their brain, in order to become what they want to become. As opposed to looking everywhere for answers, I teach people how to receive the answers from the inside because they *know*. They have everything; their brain is so powerful and there is a huge percentage of our brain that we are not even using, so it is astonishing the amount of information that we have. And even if we do seek advice and we ask everybody, and we look online, and we search for answers, and we want outside feedback, the truth is we're not going to do anything about it unless we generate the idea ourselves. Have you ever had a friend that told you, "I just got a brilliant idea to do such-and-such," and then you say to yourself, I've been telling you this for months! Everybody else has been telling them too, but now, just right now, they got the brilliant idea that they're going to do this. And it will work. They will do it because they just got the idea.

What I do is I ask the right questions to generate the lightbulbs in people's heads so that they decide for themselves, *I'm going to do this*. That's the "Think Yourself" process that I teach in my seminars. I have already published my number one best-seller, THINK Yourself™ THIN and I am currently writing THINK Yourself™ SUCCESSFUL, THINK Yourself™ WEALTHY, THINK Yourself™ a LEADER, THINK Yourself™ SEXY and THINK Yourself™ PATIENT.

It is always the same process of reprogramming your brain to be whatever you want to be. I'm creating the THINK Yourself™ movement in order for people to realize that they have everything they need inside, so there is no need to point fingers at everything that is happening to them because things are happening for them. Everything that they go through is designed to build them into the person that they are and it's all about opportunities and how to see things differently. This is what I do. That's a general picture.

"Problems are not stop signs, they are guidelines."

- Robert H. Schuller

To be more specific, some of the people I help want to lose weight. However, when they sit in my office, they realize that the reason why they have so much weight is never really because they don't know how to do a squat or they don't have enough salad recipes. It's never because they have a problem with their weight. They *know*. It's just that somehow, they hold a limiting belief that is not serving them. So we find how it's related to other things in their life. I'm not going to suggest that people cannot fix their health and fitness, but only that health and fitness are just one portion of your life. How can you focus on your health and fitness if your career asks so much of you that you have to work from 5am until 10pm? Maybe we need to work on your career, maybe your self-actualization, maybe it's your self-growth you need to work on, or your lack of self-confidence. And that's why you're gaining weight because you eat your emotions. Maybe it's love and romance. What if you're married to a person that abuses you verbally all the time? Of course it's going to impact your health and fitness.

I help people in every single one of these categories. I help people that have a hard time communicating with other people and conflicts; people like teenagers, who it is hard to communicate with sometimes. I helped a woman get pregnant, because very often they have a blockage in their heads – there's nothing wrong with them physically.

I have helped people with allergies; a lady was allergic to a cat and I helped her resolve that. I have helped people quit smoking, too. There are different reasons why people would come to my services. And ultimately, it always comes back to what are the limiting beliefs that they choose to believe about themselves that are not true and not serving them? And we replace them with something that's better, something that really serves them and makes them grow. I help people learn how to think differently.

Do you know the saying, "You can lead a horse to water but you can't make him drink?" Well, somehow, that is what is so unique about me. I can make them drink. I can ask the right questions in order to make people find within themselves what they need to be their best self. It's transformational work. When you have a broken foot, you go to the doctor, he fixes your foot, you leave, and he asks you, "How is your foot now?" and you say, "Great! Thank you." Well, when people leave my office and I ask them, "How is your foot?" they say, "What foot? I don't even remember how I used to feel." They don't remember because it's been fixed in their brain. We do some neurological pathway reprogramming so that they don't even remember how to feel sorry for themselves.

What Inspired Me to Do What I Do

There are many things that inspired me to do what I do. Firstly, two highly positive and inspiring parents raised me. At home, there were signs around the house that said, "You're awesome, you're amazing, you can do this, you're brilliant." They would always make my brother and I sit in the living room on Sundays and listen to motivational tapes. We were brainwashed very young to see life differently.

One of the stories that really inspired me as a kid was that starfish story that my parents used to tell me when I would go to bed. There was an old man on the beach throwing starfishes in the water and a little girl asks him, "What are you doing, sir?" He says, "I have to throw the starfishes back in the water, because if I don't, they're going to die on the beach." She looks around and says, "There are hundreds of starfishes on the beach. What difference is it going to make?"

Then he took one starfish and showed it to the little girl and said, "For that starfish, it makes a whole difference."

"If you can't feed a hundred people, then feed just one"

- Mother Teresa

At 6 years old, I wanted to become a starfish savior. I had to save the world one person at a time. I didn't want to be a nurse, I didn't want to be an actress; I wanted to be a starfish savior. That is when I decided to help others. In grade 7, I had a little corner in the school where my friends would meet me to go through their problems - whatever problems we can have at that age! LOL!

Events That Changed My Life

I have been in the fitness industry for a long time. I've been teaching for 29 years, and I've always been very competitive. I was using fitness as a platform to inspire as many people as possible. One year, I won Instructor of the Year for Canada, Best Fitness Instructor. My prize was to train with the best of the best in New Zealand where I spent a month. It was a wonderful experience, but when I came back I thought, *Now what? How much more can I work on myself? What is the next step? What is the next level?* Then I realized there is more to this. I didn't think I was fully living my life purpose. My life purpose cannot be being the best I can be, because in that field at that time, I felt like, *What else now?*

When I was on a trip to Barbados, I went for a run and I fell, and pulled my hamstring really badly, and my husband had to push me in a wheelchair for 3 weeks during that trip. Instead of exploring Barbados, I read books. One of the books that found its way into my hands was *A New Earth* by Eckhart Tolle, which is about the ego. I thought, *This is exactly what I needed to read right now. That's why I got injured, so that I would have time to read this book.* It's brilliant. I finally realized that I had a huge ego and I was making everything all about me, about me getting better and being the best I can be. I thought that working on myself and being the best I can be would inspire others. It did do that, to a certain extent. However, getting to the top taught me a lesson; in order to really feel that you're living your life purpose, you need to work on yourself first. You cannot help other people before liking yourself and loving yourself. There's a big difference between having a big ego and loving yourself in order to help other people. That was a big transition for me, when I turned towards other people.

"Because of its phantom nature, and despite elaborate defense mechanisms, the ego is very vulnerable and insecure, and it sees itself as constantly under threat. This, by the way, is the case even if the ego is outwardly very confident."

- Eckhart Tolle

When I discovered neuro linguistic programming in my practitioner course in Toronto about 9 years ago, I realized there was an actual technique to reprogramming people's brains. The way I had been thinking all my life, because I was introduced to it at a very young age, was teachable. I was excited to think that now I could teach people how to do it and there are actually processes to think positively and to see things differently, and get rid of negative emotion, traumas, and allergies, programming yourself to be anything you want – even pregnant. I thought: *I've got something big here.*

Overcoming Adversity

When being asked to contribute to this book, I honestly was excited about the idea to talk about adversity and had lots of ideas about the subject. I was thinking to myself, *I don't have adversity in my life but as a Life Coach, I am constantly facing it and teaching people how to go about it.*

When discussing about it with my husband, he told me, "What do you mean, you don't have adversity in your own life? Do I have to remind you that you have a brain tumour my dear?" Oops. I had kind of forgotten about it. He was right. The truth is, I've had a brain tumour for 4 years. It's honestly not a big deal to me, because nothing is, because that's the way I see things. I guess it is a big deal in the eyes of those around me though; hence the reason why I have only told a handful of people about it.

"Yesterday is not ours to recover, but tomorrow is ours to win or lose."

Lyndon B. Johnson

I could tell you about being bullied in grade 4 and 5. I had no friends; I had nobody. It's not that nothing has ever happened to me. It's just that I don't see it the same way. Of course at 9-10 years old, I had help from my parents to find a strategy that would work for me at school. They taught me to avoid saying, "Poor me, oh my gosh. The whole world is out to get me." The way I learned to approach adversity is in the way that the reason we have challenges is because they're designed to make us stronger. They're designed to teach us positive learning so that we can grow to the next level. I have to say that although a lot of people have been bullied, a lot of people have had health problems, and a lot of people go through the things that I go through. The common denominator is that challenges are not different, and everybody has a challenge. In grades 4 and 5, when I had no friends, I turned my focus on studying and spent my recess and lunch times at the library doing my homework. I was a straight A student! I am not sure if I would have been if I had not spent that much time alone. This discipline and love of learning is certainly serving me in my life now. I actually find myself loving being alone. I have my own back. It is a great feeling, knowing that you don't need anybody around to enjoy life.

"I don't need to be better than anybody or worse than anybody to feel better about myself. I just need to stick on my own path and stay in the moment as best I can."

- Marc Jacobs

Everything is a stepping-stone towards something else. If we are ill, our body sends us a message, or teaches us a way of doing things differently. I am taking strong medicine right now to get rid of this brain tumor. Could it have been prevented? I am an extremely healthy and fit person so it can't be because of my diet or my fitness. I can't say I have stress in my life. It just happened. There is no need to try and pinpoint how it happened.

How is it affecting my life? I have to go to bed at 8:30 at night because I need to sleep 10 or 11 hours a night. People think it's a choice, that I like to sleep a lot. Well, I do, but it's because I have a brain tumor. I need rest at night if I want the medicine to work. Very few people know about the brain tumour because, quite frankly, I don't want sympathy.

Everybody has stuff they go through and it's not any different for me. That's my stuff. That's what I go through.

When I was diagnosed with a brain tumour, it really surprised me. I had a new doctor and she sent me for some baseline tests and some of my hormones were out of whack and my iron was low. After a long year of tests, and even surgeries (they operated for cervical cancer as they thought that this is what I had for a while...), trying to figure out what was wrong with me, it was discovered that I have a brain tumour.

My first reaction was, *How do we fix that? What do I have to do?* It's very fortunate that it was small enough that we could treat it with strong medicine, as opposed to having to operate. So that was a blessing. Since then, it has been 4 years of that, and I'm continuing to shrink it every day by doing what I do, sending my positive vibes towards it.

See, my philosophy on physical pain is this: Our brain has a blueprint of our entire body in perfect health. Our brain heals our body all the time. When you cut yourself, you don't have to remind your skin to glue back together. Your body just does it. We heal ourselves all the time. However, sometimes, our brain sends us ideas, messages, and we don't listen. First, we receive little whispers telling us we should do such and such. If we still don't listen, our brain speaks louder and louder until, if we are still ignoring the message, he sends us a physical pain to force us to pay attention. As if our brain was going on strike on us saying: "I am telling you to do what is best for you and you are not listening, so I will stop healing you then, if you don't listen..." So, I started paying attention. What was my body trying to tell me? I have always been very busy. My sense of accomplishment drives me and makes me happy. However, I used to really spread my energy between multitudes of different things, not connected. I am a very curious person, I love to learn and I am genuinely interested in a lot of things.   I also have that belief that I can learn to be good at anything I tackle. I realized with my brain tumour that it is not because I can do something, or because I am good at it, that I should necessarily do it. I reviewed my values and what is really important to me. I am now more selective as to what I say yes to and what I take on in my life. I am still doing a million things, however, they are all connected and funnel into my life purpose. I say no to a lot of things and by knowing my top values and my life purpose - to inspire, motivate, impact and believe in myself and in people around me - it is very easy now to make decisions as to what I take on and what I let go. My body is healing itself right now, and I'm giving it all I can with healthy food, lots of sleep, no stress, staying calm, laughing a lot, and being happy.

Using My Internal Resources

There are 6 layers of your internal brain. First, we have the environment, the base. Who is around me? Surrounding myself with positive people, being in an environment where there is physically no mess. You need to tidy up your space. You need to have order in your life and to be organized. That really affects your inner self. Your environment is also the people you surround yourself with. Do you have that person in your life that drains so much energy, and you can help them to a certain point, and then all they want is an ear, to be a victim? Maybe it entails cleaning up your environment that way. Get rid of toxic friends, or chose to see them less often.

Sept 25 2023
6 layers

1. Enviroment
2. Behavior
3. Skills
4. Beliefs + Values
5. Full Identity (?)
6. Life Purpose

68

"Be careful the environment you choose for it will shape you; be careful the friends you choose for you will become like them."

- W. Clement Stone

The second layer represents your behaviour, and the things you do. You need to make sure the things you do are serving you. We only have 12-14 hours of "awake" time every day and we can choose to sit in front of the TV for 4 of them, or we can choose to do something else with our time. So use your wisdom, your power to choose, because every time we do something, we choose to do that.

Thirdly, your skills, things you're naturally good at that you want to do. You want to make sure you're using your skills, ones you have developed, the things you naturally like that you want to become better at. You might want to take courses and make sure you're using those skills.

The fourth level is your beliefs and values, what's important to you, your internal resources and self-confidence. To me, self-confidence is about 5 things: certainty, significance, growth, love and contribution.

Certainty means to be sure about something, to trust that everything that happens to you is bringing you a positive lesson, and then you can discard all of the negative emotic˺ that come with it. You just take the learning and disc˺ rest and that brings you self-confidence. Count yo˺ and be grateful if you are blessed with both your arms, your brain, your family, a ho˺

self confidence :

- certainty
- significance
- growth
- love
- contribution

to

Significance is when you feel like what you do matters. Do something that will matter for you, that is important to you, that follows your values and that you enjoy.

Growth is also necessary for self-confidence. You need to always be able to go to the next level. If you never grow, that is not how you actualize yourself and how you feel like you're living your life purpose.

Love, of course, brings self-confidence. It doesn't necessarily mean to have a significant other. You can love a lot of people in your life, even if you live by yourself. I am very blessed and lucky that I have been madly in love with my husband for 15 years. And you can love friends, family, and a lot of people, even if you're not in love, as we like to think in our society.

Contribution is important. You need to contribute to others. Once you love yourself, and you love others, then you can feel that you are contributing.

With your self-confidence, you can really be yourself and live your identity. When all the layers are aligned and you live in an environment that supports your behaviours, when your daily actions involve you using your skills and are in line with your beliefs and values, which are what is important to you, that is when you can reach your full identity and be your best. Once at the identity level, you can climb up to the sixth level: your life purpose. You can turn towards others and ask yourself, whom else am I serving? What I am here for? These are all the internal resources I use to build my self-confidence and live my life purpose.

My External Resources

I like to sleep a lot. I eat very clean, very healthy. I exercise a lot. Every day my Fitbit is counting 15,000 steps a day. That's my minimum. I love it because it tracks my sleep as well. So I can tell if I had good sleep as well, which I track more than I do my steps. It tells you if you were agitated or not. Also, you need to have family, friends, a coach—somebody you can bounce ideas off of, and I'm lucky that both of my parents are still alive and I talk to them both almost every day. My husband is very supportive of my business as well and helps me. I have fantastic friends, always there for me, and also a coach that I call when in need. My coach and I did our Masters together, and we call each other and we execute processes on each other. I can't apply a process on me that needs to be done on an unconscious level. For example, I used to be allergic to garlic, and I couldn't remove it myself, so my fellow master practitioner did it for me. There are things you can't really do at a conscious level. You have to do it on an unconscious level because it's an unconscious reaction to a problem happening at an unconscious level.

The Importance of Mindset to Overcome Adversity

Mindset is the base of everything. It's a predisposition. People can go through exactly the same things and not have the same impact. If you are adopting a victim type of mindset, everybody will be out to get you, and you will be more likely to not even pay attention to the positive things in your life. And when people are nice to you, you won't even pay attention or notice it. In your mind, everybody is out to get you, and you will only notice the bad stuff.

Get rid of the negative emotions. We put a lot of guilt on ourselves, and we feel like a failure, or that we don't know what we're doing. All that stuff is not serving us. We can say, "I'm not qualified, but I'm willing to learn how it feels to be qualified. What do qualified people think? What environment do they have around themselves? Do they surround themselves with positive, successful people? Do they read biographies of successful people?" My mom used to tell me every day, "You need to eat food consistently. You can't eat all your meals today so that you won't have to eat for the rest of the week." You go to a seminar or you read a book and you are so motivated. Two weeks later, you're back in your rut because you did not continue to feed yourself. You can't take all of your meals at once. You have to continue feeding yourself every day. Every morning, I listen to audiobooks for 15 minutes while I brush my teeth, brush my hair, and get ready for the day. During that morning preparation time, I am hearing a voice telling me I'm amazing. I chose to listen to positive, motivational stuff. I also love kids' movies. They always have a great positive lesson and they fill my mind with great images. I have no room in my head and don't feel the need to get 'polluted' with negative dramas or reality television shows. I feel that I need to continue to feed my brain. Even if I am just choosing to spend a few hours a week in front of a flat screen, my brain is always listening, so I have to be very careful what I chose to input in it.

"I'm always trying to find brain food and indulge in knowledge that's gonna be useful."

- Big Boi

5 Tips to Choosing Success Over Adversity

1. The first thing is to seek the positive learning of whatever is. Of course, you can acknowledge, "This sucks." Because if you break a leg, it sucks. If something happens to you, the first thing is to acknowledge that it is happening to you and then you say, "It's a good thing because..." and you dig until you find it. You search until you find what is the positive lesson. Maybe it's: "I'm never going to ski that fast again, I will be more careful."

    Maybe you were not well prepared for a sales pitch at work and as a result it failed terribly. You say, "That sucked. I did it. Now what have I learned from this? How is it a good thing?"

2. Then you forgive yourself. We're very upset with ourselves for doing that, and the first way to protect ourselves is to point fingers. It's got to be somebody else's fault. We have to forgive them. Sometimes it is somebody else's fault. Sometimes you are in a car accident where it is entirely somebody else's fault, so we have to forgive them. And you have to forgive yourself because you may have had something to do with it too. Once you have acknowledged it, then you forget about it and you clean up. *Now what? What is my next step? I won't repeat my mistake and what am I going to do instead? What are the steps?*

    "Forgive yourself for your faults and your mistakes and move on."

    Sept 25
    2023

    - Les Brown

3. Let it go. For good. Instead of re-living the story over and over, you're not even allowed to tell the story to anybody anymore because every time you tell the story, "...and then this happened and that happened!" ... every time you do that, your body resends all the chemicals from inside your brain and it pollutes your body with a whole bunch of negative vibes again, every single time. So forget about it. You're not even allowed to tell the story. Move on – and you do that by using your brain to decide what you're going to do. It's forward thinking. You say, "Now the next time this happens, this is what I'm going to do."

4. The system. My proprietary DNA system that I have is in three steps. The first one is to decide what it is you're going to do, "Now I want this instead." Everybody has learned how to do the planning of what they want, the vision board, but then they stop. Taking a kitchen renovation as an example, even if you have all your ideas in a folder, with all the colours you want and pictures of cupboards, tile and paint samples and a flyer showing the appliances, you aren't going to get it unless you do something about this folder. It is not enough to look at your folder, or vision board, or positive affirmation. You need two more steps. Sometimes people try and go right to the third step and they try to install the new cupboards on top of their existing cupboards and try to put the new countertop on top of the old countertop. That's not going to work. You need the middle step which is the clean-up. Gut out the old kitchen. Remove all the cupboards and the old countertops, which are the limiting beliefs, the negative emotions, all of the bad habits and bad stuff you have. Then you can go into

the third step, into re-installing the new cupboards. Once you have recognized what is happening, then you forgive yourself, you forget that happened, you let it go and you proceed with your DNA system. You elicit your desire, you clean up and then you re-install the new cupboards.

5. Use your brain. You have a personal assistant inside your head that takes notes and makes sure that everything that you say or think gets done. It's like having a waiter in your head, standing with a note pad and running to the kitchen to place your order. Whatever you think or say will get cooked by the chef and brought back to you exactly how you ordered it. So you really have to be careful when you think and when you talk. Your personal assistant is always listening. If you wake up in the morning and look at yourself in the mirror and say: "Oh my! I look horrible! I look tired!" then you continue with your day saying to yourself that you feel so stupid, or inadequate, or you don't want to be stressed and you hate rushing everywhere. You let the voice inside your head tell you that you are a failure and a fraud and you even tell yourself to not forget this (maybe a folder you are supposed to bring to the office). All your brain can hear is: Horrible, Tired, Stupid, Inadequate, Stress, Rush, Failure, Fraud, Forget the folder, etc.

If I tell you to close your eyes right now and do not visualize Mickey Mouse wearing a yellow tutu standing on top of an elephant. Did you see him? Of course you did. Even if I said, "Do Not visualize Mickey Mouse...." Your brain doesn't process negation. So you have to be careful! People sit in my office all the time telling me they don't want to be stressed anymore, they don't want to be fat, they don't want to be impatient with their kids and they don't want to be rushing all the time!

It is like they are telling their contractor that they want them to paint their kitchen "not blue." So what do you want instead? Use your brain wisely, think and say what you want, not what you don't want!

How My Brain Tumour Made Me Stronger

What really made me stronger was two years later. It's a very slow process. The tumor is small, and the doctors don't want to operate on it because why risk it if it's not growing? So they monitor it every 2 years. Because it is not frequent, I had 2 years to program myself to shrink my tumour. The biggest setback for me was not when I was diagnosed because I just thought, I have a brain tumor, I'll fix it, and when I go for my test in 2 years, it's going to be gone.

I have blood tests every 3 weeks. They monitor it that way in the meantime. When I went to my bi-annual scan, I honestly thought they would tell me I was cured. But my doctor said, "Your tumour has changed shape. It didn't grow, but it didn't get smaller either." So it didn't shrink. I thought it was gone, but it wasn't. That was a big setback for me. I thought, *Really? Are you sure?* I believed it was gone. I heal people all the time and I thought, *I can't even heal myself,* and I was pretty upset about that.

The doctor told me in some cases the medicine only keeps it from growing, and it might take 10 years before it shrinks. I have headaches once in a while and unfortunately the medicine is very addictive because if I forget to take it, I feel ill. Then as soon as I take it, it knocks me out, so I can't really go on with my day. But to be honest, it doesn't really affect me. I'm totally okay with it. People have their own stuff and go through a lot more than I do.

My two-year check-up made me stronger because I have made a lot of changes in my life and I am now acknowledging that I still need to continue to pay attention to what my brain is trying to tell me through my body. I have a very giving and generous personality. Although it serves my life purpose to help others, I am learning to take care of me first.

"When you take care of yourself, you're a better person for others. When you feel good about yourself, you treat others better."

- Solange Knowles

Sept 25
2023

My Advice For Others Going Through a Challenging Time

Trust yourself. You've got this. You have everything you need inside yourself. Stop looking for outside advice and solutions, looking up what you should do. Close your eyes and ask your unconscious mind. It knows you better than anybody else and better than your logical mind. Your logical mind can only handle on average 7 things at a time but your unconscious mind can absorb and process 2.3 million pieces of information every second. It's so powerful. It knows everything.

Your unconscious mind captures all of the non-verbal cues from every conversation you had, which are 80% of our communication. It reads every sign on the road on your way to work when you are driving. It remembers everything. It discards some, it deletes some, it distorts some to fit your reality, but it was there all your life. So don't ask people, "What should I do?" They weren't there every single moment of your life. You have all the answers and you know exactly what to do. Trust yourself. You've got this.

Don't Just Be. Be Your Best!

About the Author

Nathalie Plamondon-Thomas

DNA Life Coaching
Website: www.dnalifecoaching.ca
Email: nathalie@dnalifecoaching.com
Facebook: nathalie.plamondonthomas
Twitter: @DNALifecoaching

Nathalie Plamondon-Thomas is a Motivational Speaker, Life Coach & Executive Coach for over 10 years and the No.1 Best Selling author of 4 books on wellness and empowerment and she's working on her fifth book. Nathalie owned and operated a successful printing business for over 10 years and has over 15 years of experience in sales in the natural food industry. She is also a certified personal trainer and instructor with over 30 years of experience in the fitness industry, nutrition and wellness specialist and weight loss. Nathalie combines her sales strengths with the concepts of motivation and the brain programming processes she practices as a Master in Neuro Linguistic Programming. Nathalie is an amazing positive thinker who believes that everybody has whatever he or she needs inside their DNA in order to obtain, achieve and be whatever they put their mind to. More than a company mission statement, her life purpose is to motivate and inspire others to be their best.

"You can take a horse to water but you can't make him drink...' Somehow, Nathalie can.

Chapter 5:

Aligning With Your Core

By Kim Standeven

Kim is a healer, and a wholehearted person who strives to offer a space for people to be the best version of themselves. She inspires people to have the courage to be authentic and to live in alignment with who they are. She invites her clients and workshop participants to dream big and push past the fears and doubts that creep in and stop us from moving forward.

Kim inspires others because she had the courage to get vulnerable and commit to doing the work needed to heal and succeed in life. She's faced heart wrenching challenges and walked through them with grace and perseverance. Kim has a great gift for connecting with people at a deep and profound level. She has the ability to see you for who you are and your potential for greatness. She takes the time and genuinely cares about your success and wellbeing. Kim tends to leave a lasting impression with her quiet leadership and questions that stay with us long after gently mentoring and inspiring us along the way.

Helping Others

My passion is working as a life coach, workshop facilitator, speaker and author. I call myself a Core Alignment Coach because I help people align with the core of who they are, their authentic self, by exploring their deepest held values and desires. Through my work, I help people who have a desire for more in their life and who are asking themselves questions and are curious about the path that they're on. The majority of my clients are women who are drawn to the helping professions. They are spiritually connected to our universe, have a deep love of learning and a great desire to grow. I have noticed that most people who help others rarely take the time for themselves. They're so focused on healing and helping that they forget about their own wellbeing. I take great satisfaction and pride in coaching those who dedicate their energy and life to helping others as leaders, healers or teachers.

As a coach, I provide my clients dedicated time to fill up their emotional and spiritual tank and offer a safe space to do that. We live in a very distracted world so it is crucial to offer an outlet for shutting out all the noise. What I mean by noise is the expectations, the judgments, the should's ("I think I should do this") so that they can make decisions from an internal, authentic, core place rather than making decisions based on the external 'should do' or 'expected to do' perspective.

I offer people the opportunity to access clarity. A chance to connect to what they really think and feel without external noise. The coaching conversation allows us to solve the problem of confusion, disconnection from yourself, self-doubt and lack of confidence. I help others answer the question many of us face in our life: "What's my purpose? Who am I? What's next for me?" I help to clear out the distraction, clutter and offer people an opportunity to access the answers to those questions for themselves by tapping into their inner wisdom.

As a compassionate and deep feeling teenager, I knew I wanted to help people but I didn't know in what way. I noticed I really enjoyed studying psychology so that's what I focused on in my university years. I was curious about what made us tick as humans. Why we did the things that we did. After I graduated, I didn't feel like my education quite fit me, so I decided to go off into the world after university and explore. I'm so blessed that I did that because I chose to live a little and I ended up finding my way organically. I worked for nearly 15 years in various leadership positions in the corporate world which helped me realize my passion is personal development.

When My Life Changed

My life changed at 14 years old in a flash and with a single sentence uttered by my father. I was standing in the kitchen with him when he said "Kim, I can't see." After a series of tests, doctors and agonizing waiting, it was discovered that Dad had suffered from a brain AVM (cluster of blood vessels) that haemorrhaged. It completely rocked my world. He was only 42 years old and required invasive brain surgery to repair the bleeding. The surgery repaired the AVM and saved his life but the damage was insurmountable. He was left severely disabled and confined to a wheelchair. He lost most of the freedoms many of us take for granted such as speaking, walking, sight, and coordination. He was as vulnerable as a baby and needed 24-7 care. I lost myself in this very tragic experience, drowning in grief for losing my hero and feeling like I had to become his parent rather than his daughter. When I look back on those years, I was merely living on autopilot, completely numb and putting on a smile to please the world. I did everything to ignore my pain, stuffing it down deep until I was in my late 20's when I started to realize I didn't want to live in my numb state anymore. It felt hollow and I started asking myself deep, vulnerable questions and I knew I needed help. I knew I needed to heal and move past this tragedy in my life not only for myself but for my dad.

As a 30 year old young women desperate to find answers and break free from my past pain, I started with a simple intention: *"Please send me someone to help me heal."* I thought and said this over and over and then there she was; I will never forget the moment I met Lori Anne and the opportunity to learn the art of coaching. A colleague of mine was doing a presentation at a workshop I was at, and she was teaching us the beautiful process of coaching. I went up to her feeling so inspired and I said, "You have to tell me more about this. What is coaching? Where did you learn this skill?" She was thrilled and said, "Actually Lori Anne, the lady who taught me, is putting on a course in a couple of months. You should contact her." I emailed her and told her I wanted to sign up. I never even thought about it. I just immediately knew it was perfect. I didn't care how much it was and I didn't even know how I was going to pay for it. I would find a way, I just had to do it. I had a clear knowing that I had to become a coach but not any coach; a Core Alignment Coach with Lori Anne Demers. There was no hesitation and no doubt when I heard about her program, I just said yes. I knew my life was going to change forever, I knew I was finally on the road to healing. Lori Anne was my mentor and teacher. She taught me what living authentically meant. She not only taught me how to coach but she taught me how to heal myself by getting vulnerable and letting go. The biggest lesson I learned in my coach training was that I had to know myself first before attempting to support others. I took this very seriously. She pushed and challenged me but most importantly she believed in me. I had been asking the universe for a long time for some help and in that moment I knew this was the help I was seeking. I needed to become a coach and she was the woman I needed to learn from.

When I look back, I feel immensely grateful that I trusted my intuition. I trusted my inner voice that said "Yes, do it," because now I get to help others learn how to trust their own inner knowing. I have the best job!

What Drives My Passion

My passion is a fire of desire within and it all starts with me. I wake up every day striving to be the best version of myself. My drive is sparked by that lesson of knowing myself first. I dedicate much of my time continuing to develop myself so that I can share what I've learned to inspire and support others. It is imperative that I focus on doing the work I need to do to remain aligned, whole and content.

I feel really fulfilled. It fills me up when I connect with people on a very deep and profound level. As a coach, people share with me their innermost deepest thoughts and I've had many people say, "I share with you stuff that I don't even share with my closest family, friends or even my spouse. You know things about me that nobody else on earth knows." I take that very seriously. I'm immensely honoured to be the keeper of these deep-felt thoughts and desires. The depth and connection I experience with my clients is what drives me; the fact that I give people that space to say whatever is on their mind without any judgment or advice is immensely rewarding. I don't want people to live in that numb state that I did for so many years. I don't want other people to live like I was living because it's really not living. I think we all deserve to experience ourselves at our fullest potential. We deserve that and that's why I do what I do. This is what drives me - the possibility of us achieving our potential, our dreams.

Getting Started Coaching

I began coaching when I worked in the corporate world. I became a certified coach and pitched to my boss that I think this process is incredible and can I offer it to leaders within the organization. At the time, I was a Leadership Advisor so coaching was a natural fit for my position. I started coaching managers and leaders all across Canada and got very comfortable with the process. I enjoyed my time in the corporate world but the little voice inside was always saying 'this isn't forever. You are meant to do more." One day my voice said "Kim, it's time. It's time to go out there on your own and share your story and share your message. I know it's scary but it's time." I took the leap and said, "I'm going to start my own business," and that's what I did.

Fear of Stepping Out

No one ever came out and said "I think you're nuts for starting a business." I think I was probably the hardest on myself, often getting sucked into moments of doubt but I always brought myself back to why I had a desire to become a coach in the first place. I brought myself back to that moment of when I didn't hesitate and said yes. There were and are times I think I am a little nuts but I have a really great network of people, family and friends who are always cheering me on. I think what was really great about stepping out is that people saw that it was my dream and wanted to support the fact that dreams are worth working hard for. I've never had anyone say, "I don't think you should be doing this." My mom is my biggest fan, my brother was my first coaching client and even my husband who I know doesn't completely understand what I do always trusts me to do what I think is best. The fear of stepping out loosens it grip when you have a community of people who believe in you and when you believe in yourself.

Overcoming Adversity

I think the word I would use to describe the adversity I faced is grief. I had to first identify the fact that I was stuck in grief and then find my way out of the long dark tunnel grief cocooned me in. I lost myself in my father's medical tragedy. He had a brain haemorrhage. I had to accept this reality. My dad was no longer the man I had once known. I had to learn how to connect with him again despite all his physical challenges. As a teenager, trying to navigate my own identity became complicated because my identity got entangled in the heartache. I started to identify myself as the daughter of a disabled father rather than Kim, an independent, intelligent, young woman. I was grieving the loss of the dad that I thought I deserved. I was in that tunnel of grief and feeling angry at the world. It took me over 20 years to figure out what it meant to be me outside of this tragic experience.

I needed to figure out not only how to move through grief but more specifically how to separate who I am from what I experienced. I finally realized that what we experience is not who we are. I was never taught that very important distinction.

I was only 14 years old at the time and it was hard enough trying to figure out where I fit in the world. The adversity I faced was compounded because I was dealing with several tragic events in my life at a time when I was just starting to figure what it meant to be me.

My parents divorced only two years before my dad's hemorrhage occurred so it was a very lonely time for me. And to add another level of complexity, my mom got sick at the exact same time as my dad. My mom was dealing with chronic migraines to the point that she was bedridden for years.

So, imagine a 14-year-old girl with both parents seriously ill and trying to figure out life. I felt very alone and also a sense of responsibility to grow up fast. I decided that I needed to be 'strong' because both my parents were in crisis. I stuffed my emotions and put on a smile. Ignoring my pain was very, very damaging. That decision put me on the path of living in a numb state for way too many years. I was stuck in the tunnel of grief.

Waiting For Something Bad to Happen

When I think about what these past experiences impacted; it changed my view of the world. I compare it to putting on a pair of glasses. I made a decision to change the lenses I had in the glasses. I chose lenses that were very hazy, dark, and cloudy and I brought that perspective into all of my experiences. I believed in a very damaging belief. I believed that 'bad things happen to good people.' Therefore, life should be feared. That's how I chose to see the world and it impacted my thoughts and experiences.

I was waiting for something bad to happen all the time. Both my parents were unable to actively participate in life because of illness. I was very angry and I decided that life was a trick, I didn't want to take risks, and I was debilitatingly careful all the time. I was afraid to wake up in the morning because I didn't have control over what was going to happen. My dad woke up one day and said, "I can't see". My mom woke up one day and couldn't get out of bed. Life felt very negative and dark. I was entangled in my negativity but at the same time there was always a little voice inside whispering that it didn't have to be this way. Life is worth living without fear. This voice started to become stronger and louder.

I started to slowly walk out of my tunnel, after being on autopilot for so many years. I realized that what I needed to do was change the lenses in my glasses. I learned that I had a choice and I could re-train my brain with the thoughts I was thinking. I immersed myself in the study of psychology and coaching and I was introduced to these wonderful things called neural pathways in our brain. In order to heal and create the life I desired all I needed to do was create new neural pathways in my brain. Coaching offered me a process to create them through conversation and commitment. That is how I got through it. I did the work.

I created new stronger pathways. I shifted the negativity and the damaging beliefs into a positive vision for my life. It took and takes a lot of daily work because our brains are naturally wired to hold onto to what's familiar. I continuously shift negative thoughts by saying to myself, "No, that's not what I want or who I am." I learned how and the reason I am a coach is because I want to help others do the same.

It Takes Time

It took me nearly 25 years to get where I am today – one step at a time. It's not something that ever ends. Every day I have to wake up and make a conscious choice to accept my life and to seek the positive in it. Every single day I choose what neural pathways I want to work on. It's like exercising the muscles in my body. I have to decide which ones I want to strengthen because it would be so easy to get sucked back into the grief. It's always there – it never really goes away – so it's a choice. I have to see my experiences as an opportunity to learn from rather than live as a victim.

What Got Me Through

My family teases me that I am a bit stubborn which I can't deny. Yes, I am passionate and determined. I think these attributes actually helped me. I was and am determined to never give up. My connection with my dad and my mom is what got me through. My dad motivates me even though he's no longer here in body since he passed 17 years after his brain surgery. I feel like he's with me and he's tapping me on the shoulder here and there reminding me of what is important. He encourages me with the lessons he passed on and I want to honour him and his legacy. The experience with my dad was very profound but my mom also showed such incredible strength in her own health journey and she continues to be my greatest teacher in my life. I want to honour both of them in my actions and in the choices I make. They remind me what is important and for that I am grateful.

The support I received from my family and friends really helped me stay true to what I wanted to create and sometimes I needed their cheerleading in the moments when I wanted to give up. When I started on my journey of healing I think they knew what I was doing was powerful because they experienced me differently. When I started my own business, they knew what I was doing was really important to me because of my passion and dedication to it. What really surprised me was the role my clients have played in my journey. With each client I connect with I am blessed with more insights, healing and growth. My clients have incredible wisdom and what they share with me has been a great gift for my own development.

What also got me through was my commitment to learning and studying. My love of learning serves as a security blanket. In a way, it offered me a place to explore and access the wisdom I needed in order to move forward. One other very important support that helped me was my connection with nature. I feel very fortunate to live surrounded by nature so whenever I feel I'm off track I take some time to go outside to get grounded and centered. Taking the time to connect with the people in my life, my desire to learn and being in nature is all I need to get through the ups and downs.

The Importance of Mindset

Mindset is the key to overcoming adversity because in order for you to stay aligned with your core you need to work at it, every single day. It's so easy to get pulled off track and get caught up in all of the noise and distraction. In order to focus and create the life we desire we need support, clarity and commitment. We have to continually catch ourselves in the negative narrative and shift into a positive, creative and authentic way of being. We need to explore, get vulnerable, honest and ask, "Is my current mindset working for me?" It all starts with questions and a willingness to explore and define who we are.

When I wake up in the morning I ask myself this question – "Who do I want to be?" Throughout my day, I ask "Am I aligned with who I want to be?" This is the foundation for the life I am creating and a choice I get to make in all of my interactions.

5 Tips to Choosing Success Over Adversity

1. Make a Choice. It starts with you. You have the ability to make choices and you have to choose success over being stuck in adversity. It is crucial to shift your thinking and see your adversity from another perspective.

2. Get Clear. Define and get clear about what success means for you. Without a definition or a clear vision of what success is you'll just wander aimlessly. Clarity is essential and is the key. How will you know when you are successful? What does success look and feel like?

3. Create support structures. We need a structure to keep us on track. For example, a structure could be as simple as meeting with a coach every month or a community of like-minded people. You have to build systems around you to keep the momentum going and to minimize being pulled off track into the distractions.

4. Re-train your Brain. Our brain needs to be worked out. The same way we work on our muscles we need to work on strengthening our neuro-pathways. Our thoughts create our reality and those positive thoughts need to be strengthened every day or the pathways will shrivel up and die – literally.

5. Align with your Core. Figure out who you are at your core and what it means to be aligned because when you make decisions from an authentic place you will always be on the right path.

What I went through with my dad and mom made me stronger because I know what I stand for and I know what I want and I know who I am. I know what my dreams are and I know that they're possible. I feel more alive and more connected than I ever have. I feel more aligned to who I am and I'm free, therefore I am stronger.

I'm free because I am no longer weighed down by others. I'm free from carrying everybody else's opinion and judgments. I'm in a place where I can let go of all that and be who I am and love it. I'm stronger because I can look somebody in the eye and think *"It's okay that you don't agree or we have a different opinion. I'm going to do what I feel is best for me but thank you for your thoughts."* I can live authentically and I can do it with grace. I no longer stuff my emotions. I feel all of it and I share it. That's what I think strength is, being able to stand in your own authentic self.

How I Changed

I feel like I remembered who I'm meant to be. I woke up from my numb zombie-like state and I remembered what my gifts are and this changed my view on life. I think who we are at our core is with us at birth until we die so I don't think that changes. What I think happened for me is that I remembered. I woke up.

This was really a great gift because I got to a place where I am proud to be me. I love who I am, I love the experiences I have had and I wouldn't want it any other way.

An Important Lesson I Learned

My dad woke up one morning and said he couldn't see and everything changed. It changed our entire life and in that moment and every single moment since then I feel grateful for the fact that I'm here on the earth. I'm grateful for the little things. I don't know what the future will bring and it doesn't matter because as long as I focus on what matters to me today and in this moment, I know the future will be bright.

What I learned from my dad in his medical tragedy was that you can't take anything for granted because you don't know what's going to happen when you wake up in the morning. You have to be present and grateful for today. That's what I learned and that's how I live my life. If there's something that I want to do, I do it. My dad was 42 years old when his life changed forever. In an instant, he wasn't able to do the things that he loved to do because of his brain injury. If you want to go ride a motorcycle, go ride the motorcycle. If you want to write a book, write the book. Start.

If You Are Going Through a Challenging Time

Allow yourself to feel all of it. Give yourself permission to be in whatever place you're in. Give yourself space to explore the experience fully and then when you're ready, get curious. Be a student of your experiences. I tell myself all the time: "Be an archaeologist of your experience." Be willing to dig a little deeper. If you can imagine yourself rising above whatever you're going through in your life and looking at it from a neutral perspective ask yourself - "What do you see, feel, experience? What is there to learn? What can you take away to be better? What did it teach you?"

The other piece of advice I would give is to get help and support. There's so many incredible people in this world offering different ways to heal and to explore. Ask yourself: What do I need in order to move through this in a healthy way? That's the key word – healthy. What do I need in order to move through this in *a healthy way* and then see what bubbles up to the surface?

You never know who may show up in your world, just like Lori Anne did for me. I immediately knew that I needed to be with this woman. She was the person that I needed to help me heal. Notice who is crossing your path, notice the messages that you're getting. Is there a reason you are reading this particular book? Which story resonates with you? The answer is there waiting for you to notice. Sept 25/23

Trust your inner wisdom. I believe we will truly be successful when we align with who we are. Life is meant to flow like the current of the river so we need to ask ourselves are we fighting to go upstream and if we are we need to look at that because we're meant to flow with ease.

Our struggles are a big sign for us so take notice because they can serve as course corrections in our life. The adversity is trying to push us to where we need to go. Get curious, start asking questions and listen to your core.

About the Author

Kim Standeven

www.kimstandeven.com
Facebook: /kimstandevencoach
kimstandevencoaching@gmail.com
Phone: 204-208-4313
Amazon: Standeven

Kim Standeven ACC, BA works as a Core Alignment Life Coach supporting individuals, groups and organizations. Kim is the author of the best-selling book *Stand Even: A mentorship memoir. A mentorship philosophy.* Her passion and purpose is to partner with people to empower them to create a life that is aligned with their true authentic self.

For over a decade, she has put into practice her combined education in Coaching, Psychology and HR, along with years of mentorship, training and hands on experience which has enabled her to witness people transform their careers, relationships and self-worth. Kim's compassionate, open and supportive style creates an environment for her clients to succeed.

Chapter 6:

Living Your Greatest Potential

By Tasha Hughes

Tasha Hughes is a Big Picture person with a strong vision for a world in which everyone LIVES their greatest potential. Her programmes, Diva Defence and The Neuroscience of Thriving, facilitate radical growth through cognitive fitness, community and fun! Tasha has been working in the Health and Fitness industry for the last 25 years. She is a Black Belt in Karate, Yoga Teacher, Health and Fitness Coach, Speaker, Seminar Facilitator, and presently launching her lifestyle website, "Living a Gorgeous Life @ Tasha Hughes".

Diva Defence is a hybrid of yoga, martial arts, and self-empowerment for women. It is the fitness expression of the other leg of her business, The Neuroscience of Thriving, which is the science of how we intentionally shift away from the mediocre and move towards more optimal states of thriving and excellence.

About My Business

I help my students and clients first and foremost by really 'seeing' them for who they are, both the bruises and the brilliances. Often my clients have said that they just need to 'get back to who they are'. Sometimes they have been a working Mom and wife, or single Mom, for so long and dedicated to the people around them, they want to become reacquainted with lost parts of themselves. Sometimes, life has fallen apart. Maybe they are grieving life's dreams that didn't come to fruition. These women are needing to pick themselves up and/or re-invent themselves, and move forward in a really radical way. For these women, my programme is transformational, inspirational and motivational in the nicest kick-ass way possible. They tell me that I am a good listener, and someone they can count on to hold the best vision of who they are, until they can see it for themselves.

What Inspired Me To Do What I Do

The seeds to the present incarnation of my business were planted many years ago, five minutes after I finished my black belt endurance test for Karate. The test is designed to push you past your comfort zone physically, but more importantly, emotionally and mentally as well. I realized in those moments following, that I would never go down without a fight, in any situation in my life. I would always have my own back, and stand up for what I believed was right. As a woman, it is incredibly powerful to know with absolute certainty that I will have the courage and tenacity when I need it the most, to make the best choices for yourself.

What Drives Me

Like many people, I have grieved the loss of a life that did not unfold as I had hoped. Like many people, I have suffered the loss of a dream. We can, however, CHOOSE to be transformed by past experiences, and not imprisoned by them. THAT drives me – to help other people pick themselves up, brush themselves off and use those experiences to build strength and character. Then it is possible to either revisit old dreams or create new ones with the added benefit of life experience and wisdom.

I have always been a bit of a maverick. Anybody who knows me well is not surprised when I am fueled by a new or innovative approach to my areas of expertise and interest. I have made it my business to surround myself with people who are supportive and encouraging. None of us can advance our hopes and dreams without it. At times, that has meant that I have had to do a little 'weeding out'. Every relationship is for a reason, a season or a lifetime, and one of the great skills of life is being able to discern which is which.

A Major Period of Adversity

Looking back, I could call it the Sweet and Sour Chapter of my life. It is not one event, but a series of events over a 6-year period, bookended by the birth of my son at one end and the ending of my marriage at the other.

The birth of our son had once again filled our home and marriage with sweetness, preceded by the presence of my stepsons who are 8 and 10 years older than our third. All 3 boys are the SWEETness in this chapter, and my intense love for them was the motivating force behind my determination to survive the rest.

Three months after our youngest was born, my husband's Mother passed away after a lengthy illness and hospital stay. In the three years following, we would lose 2 more parents, one of which was a cancer patient requiring round-the-clock care in our home. Six months after our son's birth, we found ourselves facing a situation where the eldest boys would potentially be moved 3 hours away from us and their baby brother. The thought of losing them, amidst all of this, was heart-wrenching.

Adding to this, the market crash of 2008 destabilized the economy, job loss was rampant, and our businesses, almost entirely reliant on employee healthcare benefits, saw a rapid loss. This disrupted our businesses and lifestyle as we had known it for many years. As a result, my then husband took a teaching job out of town, and my focus shifted entirely to trying to be the best Mom and wife I could be. With all of the stress, I was constantly plagued by feelings of guilt that I was not able to be the care-free Mommy I wanted our son to have. To add to all of it, we also moved twice during that 6-year period.

Ultimately, our marriage did not survive all of the adversity. When you speak to people who have been married 40+ years, they will often refer to periods of discord during their marriage, but what made them stronger as a couple was staying committed to the bigger picture. I did not want the loss of our marriage. Not for the older boys who had already been through it once, not for our son, and not for us.

I had waited until later in life to get married, hoping that in doing so, I could somehow insulate all of us against a bad outcome. I eventually had to come to grips with the fact that I could not save us all.

Certain events such as deaths and the market crash were completely out of our control. As far as my commitment to the family, I can say in all honesty that I could have done nothing more. We took our time talking about the separation, we went to counselling, albeit I was far more invested in this process than my husband. I was hopeful very many times during those two years that we might put the proverbial wheels back on the bus. I can now stand in my own integrity and say I left no stone unturned in working toward a resolution.

I felt shame and embarrassment when our marriage ended because we were one of *those couples*. People would say that we were that couple that a lot of people looked to, that seemed to have it all together. For many years, we did. We had the workings of a really good friendship and a really good marriage and a really good relationship. It just became taxed by one too many of life's challenges. I felt like a failure.

It turned our lives completely upside down. We had chosen to focus on my husband's teaching career over mine, which held more promise in terms of pensions, retirement and benefits. The subsequent separation meant that not only was I the primary caregiver but I had to try to find stable footing for my own work life outside of what had been our home clinic.

Our entire routine needed to be rewired to continue to support my ex-husband's teaching schedule, coupled with our son now having to divide his time between Mom and Dad's houses. Of course, he too had also suffered tremendous change and loss during those years, which we can sometimes forget when children are young.

Overcoming the Pain and Adversity

Ultimately, love is the driving force behind everything I do. My love for the kids had propelled me forward and kept me committed to not falling apart, because I knew they were looking to us and how we were going to manage this. They were looking to see how resilient we might be, and that would, in some way, shape their ability to manage the mess. It was not perfectly executed. In retrospect there are things I could have handled much better, but I always tried to move forward with the right intentions.

Love has always been my highest motivator. I'm devoted to being a really good mom. I have an amazing mom, who was single at a time in history when there really weren't single moms. I learned from watching her at a very early age what it means to stop, pause, gather into yourself, and make decisions about what your priorities are and what the big picture is going to look like for yourself and your children. As a child, I believe I internalized a lot of her processes. When I needed it most, that knowledge was already available to me. Of course, she was there for me in person to talk me through it as well.

One of the things I remember saying to her was, "I didn't get married late in life because I wanted to be a statistic. I don't want to be a divorce statistic." And she looked at me and said, "Everybody is a statistic. Whether you're married, separated, divorced, or you have red hair. It doesn't matter—you're some sort of a statistic. Don't hang your identity from this point

forward on that very limited interpretation of yourself."
Those wise words fueled my positivity in terms of moving
forward in a good way.

I also had some really great friends who were also going
through it simultaneously. I stayed committed to preserving
the innocence of our youngest, as well as my own. I did not
want to become bitter, angry and cynical as a result of the
adversity, so every day I had to choose how I was going to
shift my focus, while still remaining authentic to my own
emotional journey.

That period of adversity ended three-and-a-half years ago.
Whoever said it takes only a year is a stronger person than I
am! I finally feel like I am at the end of the tunnel.

Pulling From My Internal Resources

Love, devotion to being a good Mom, resiliency gifted to me
by my Mom, honesty, a commitment to my own emotional
process, mischief, playfulness and grit are my most
frequented resources.

The memory of going through my Karate black belt test, even
years later, gave me the courage to just "be" with the fear and
the grief and the disappointment. "To do" the task at hand, to
put one foot in front of the other. Becoming a black belt in
Karate taught me so much. The training took about 7 years.
Early on in my training, because of an injury, I had been told
I would never go back into the dojo. I decided that I didn't
like that answer, so I found a woman who was an
acupuncturist. She had been a western trained medical
physician for most of her life and decided that she wanted to

focus on the source of the problem, and became an acupuncturist instead. She said, "Yes, you can do this. I'm going to treat you for 6 hours. You're going to feel like you've been hit by a truck for about 3 days, then I'm going to give you rehab for about 6 months," which she did, and then after that I was able to work through it and eventually get my black belt. The final year of training between brown and black, I was training 2-3 hours a day 6 days a week. I lived to train.

At that time, I did not have kids. At that time I was single so I had the luxury of time to be able to devote to it. I'm really glad that I did. Going into the black belt test, you have to know what you're doing, you have to know what you've been taught, you have to practice, and you have to have endurance.

Five minutes after my endurance test I came off the floor, and completely fell apart. I was joyful, I was relieved, I was exhausted. And I had a thought moving forward, *You will always have your own back. You will never let yourself down.* And as a woman, that's a pretty powerful realization to come to. No one told me to expect that.

When I tell that story to groups of women, it resonates with them. That experience has fueled me through so many challenges in my life because I think back on it and I think, *I've got this.* It might not look pretty. Is it going to look finessed? No, not always. Am I always going to be 100% sure about what I'm doing? Not always. Sure, there is a lot of doubt and second guessing, and hard work that goes into it, but ultimately, I know I'm not going to let myself down. I attribute so many times in my life back to that particular time of the endurance test. There was no way of getting through it other than to go through it. That's just it.

Over the years, I have come to trust that the only way to deal with fear is *through* it. In yoga I also I learned to "sit with it", and if you sit with it long enough and just allow it to be what it is, transformation WILL happen. If we fight it, or divert it, or try to escape it—it stays until it teaches us what we need to know.

What Helped Me Get Through It

During our talks of separation, I was undergoing parts of the yoga teacher training, the intensity of which was entirely cathartic for me. That gave me an amazing community, a spiritual focus and a physical practice to move the emotions.

Meditation helped me too, as well as my Mom, good friends, and of course my young son with the big personality!

The Importance of Mindset to Overcoming Adversity

Mindset is everything. My favourite quote when I was studying the neurosphysiology of meditation is by Victor Frankl. He said:

"Between the <u>stimulus</u> and the <u>response</u> is a space. In that space is our power to choose our response. In our response lies our growth and our freedom."

In yoga, we talk about the pause between the inhalation and the exhalation. In that pause the yogis say is where you will meet yourself, both your greatest fears and your highest potential. When we go to the yoga mat, we have an opportunity to invite both the fears and the joys to be transformed into compassion and action. Every act begins with a thought, and therefore a healthy mindset is crucial to a healthy life.

My Signature Talk that I give at events is called The Power of the Pause. Whenever we stop to pause, we have the ability to make a choice. So between whatever we are challenged by and the time we respond, we can choose to stop, to pause, and say, "What am I going to fill the pause with? Am I going to fill it with fear or self-doubt or am I going to fill it with courage and love, and things that are positive?" Whenever we choose to fill the pause with something positive, there is always a positive outcome.

We can all look back at times in our life where we have done something that was motivated by a bad intention. In my experience, if I start out with a bad intention, it never ends well for me and oftentimes not for other people. But if we stop and say, "In this present moment, I can take the time to stop, to inhale, to consider what I want the outcome to be and then on the exhalation, release the things that are not going to serve me moving forward." Then we can decide what the best step is for our forward growth, in keeping with the highest vision we have for ourselves and the people around us. Oftentimes, when we ask those questions in that pause, when we ask empowered or courageous questions, the answers we get back will resonate with the truth of who we truly are on the inside.

We all play it small. It's safe and comfortable. But when we stop and pause and ask those questions, we respond from the biggest version of ourselves. And I think when we do that, we feel good about it. It bolsters our ability to do it the exact same way whenever we have another question. We stop, we reset, we choose, and then we do it again. Every time we do that, we gain more and more momentum and more and more courage to be able to step up and live more fully.

5 Tips to Choosing Success Over Adversity

1. Be authentic and true to your feelings.

2. Sit with the discomfort. It is how we grow and how transformation happens.

3. "Weed out". If it does not support you in a healthy way, it does not belong.

4. Choose healthy influences – books, friends, movies, conversations, music...

5. Train your Mind to see the positive. It will keep you motivated and on task.

What I Can Offer to Others

Life is full of change and surprises. The only thing we have any control over is ourselves; our actions and our reactions. My humble offering is this:

Give yourself permission to feel whatever it is that you're feeling. We don't get through to the other side without feeling it. Yes, it's very scary, and that's why the next step is to make sure you've got really solid support around you. Figure out who the naysayers are in your life and get rid of them. I think we've all had the experience where life falls apart and then suddenly, we realize some of the people we thought were supporting us are actually a little bit happy about our failure. Sometimes you realize people come out of the woodwork to support you in ways that you just didn't anticipate.

We are all too hard on ourselves. Give yourself permission to be where you're at, to sit with that sense of failure or shame, or those negative feelings that come up for all of us. Take stock, look around, and ask who is going to help you to get through this. Be open and receptive to the help that will sometimes come from places that you weren't expecting. Once we're surrounded by support and not by people who would like to see us fall down, then we can start to make solid choices, and start to take inspired actions. One step at a time, one day at a time, or sometimes it's one minute at a time.

Be careful with what you distract yourself with. We're all going to be looking for escapes during those times, so again, it comes back to finding a positive escape rather than a negative one. Be kind to yourself. As women, we have a tendency to really beat ourselves up and feel we have to look and act and be perfect in every moment. Sometimes it's in letting the thing fall apart that we find talents we didn't even realize were there.

About the Author

Tasha Hughes

www.tashahughes.com
buddhabrainyoga@gmail.com

Tasha Hughes has worn multiple hats in the Health, Fitness and Wellness Industry over the last 25 years. A Black Belt in Karate, Yoga Teacher, Women's Empowerment Coach, Seminar Facilitator, and Author, she also studied Journalism at Carleton University, Spanish at Universidad de Autonoma in Madrid, Spain, World Religions at the University of Waterloo, as well as Independent Studies on the Neurophysiology Of Meditation.

Until the breakdown of her marriage, Tasha had been lucky and successful at everything she set her mind to. The end of that relationship marked the end of a "charmed life" in many ways, as she had to face the shame and sense of failure that it created. It was then that all of her beliefs, skills and knowledge would be tested. It was THE true test of all she claimed to live by. It was also the event that ultimately set her on her present course, to authentically work with women, and create environments in which they could redefine themselves after their own perceived "failures" in life.

In 2017, Tasha is preparing "Sexy, Playful and Strong: Redefining Yourself After Life Falls Apart", an offshoot of Diva Defence, as well as co-authoring another book "Think Yourself Successful". Tasha believes that success is an inside job; our inner work is

VITAL to our outer experience, and that we can grab hold of the reins and design a life that is uniquely ours to design.

Tasha's Motto: "I win or I Learn."

Chapter 7:

The Power of Passion & Persistence

By Pascale Hansen

Pascale Hansen works in the financial services industry helping companies get and remain profitable by providing customized risk strategies and solutions. Pascale also works as a life strategist helping people achieve their dreams which usually require some financial strategies to make them happen, and that's where Pascale excels. She gets excited about helping people and that's why she is so good at what she does.

Why I Love Helping People Grow Their Businesses

A statistic that I just heard recently, which I found staggering, was about female entrepreneurs: 70% of them fail because of their lack of financial literacy, which is really sad. There are so many creative and talented women working extremely hard to live their entrepreneurial dream and the only reason they're failing is because they don't know what they don't know. They don't know how important it is to actually know the fundamentals, the numbers, the inherent risks in business and how to achieve and maintain healthy cash flow.

If you want to create a sustainable business, you need to know enough about legal and financial risks to be able to delegate the responsibility to experts. It's not an unnecessary expense but an investment in the longevity of your business to get the right people on board. In general, men and women combined, we know that the odds of your business being around 10 years from now, as a business that starts today, is about 4%. And that's being around, not necessarily being profitable.

The fundamentals of money management and wealth creation haven't changed, in business and personal finance alike. It's really about education and learning what strategies will help you meet your financial goals, but who takes the time to teach you? My parents knew about money but they didn't teach me. If I had learned about money matters in my teens and early twenties and knew half of what I know today, I could have retired 20 years ago! The only thing I remember learning was that you always had to save some money. So I was a good saver; I would save half of my paycheque but that's just not enough. Ideally, your money will be working for you and growing at a pace that will ensure your specific and measurable goals will be achieved. I learned late in life, but now I get a lot of personal satisfaction from earning my living helping businesses and families get financially fit.

The Importance of Being Connected

I think most people would say I'm a good friend and I'm very well-connected. I often get phone calls saying, "You know a lot of people. Do you think you can help me with XYZ?" I got a call from a friend recently who was trying to get gloves at wholesale prices because he wanted to take them to a homeless shelter during an unseasonably cold winter. My friend asked me, "Do you know somewhere I could get wholesale gloves?" And then it suddenly hit me that a past prospect of mine was a glove company, so I called the CFO to see if they had any gloves lying around. I wanted to see if I could get gloves for free so that my friend could save the money earmarked for gloves and buy other warm clothing or food and make his budget go further. Thankfully, the CFO of the glove company arranged to have enough gloves for everyone at the homeless shelter and they were ready for pick up the next day. I do get a lot of random calls for help and I'm always happy to reach out to my network to help people for business or personal projects. I'm also extremely fortunate to know a lot of very generous, supportive people. I meet a lot people every week and as my network grows, I always try to keep in mind how I can be of service to everyone I know and meet. If I can't help someone personally, I'll always try to find someone who can.

My Inspiration to Make the Decision to Do What I Do

I grew up in a very dysfunctional family. I remember being very young, less than 3, and watching my parents have very ugly fights and doing things no child should see. I remember thinking, "Why are they doing this? Do they know that I'm here?" From that moment, I was always curious about why people do what they do.

That led to me getting a degree in psychology. I loved my studies and I developed a strong desire to help people improve their lives but I knew that being a psychiatrist with the many years of schooling required or being a psychotherapist wasn't really what I wanted to do. I did learn that despite the talents and potential of an individual, you can't give people intrinsic motivation. That's something that comes from within, so I never wanted to be in a profession where I felt compelled to work with everyone that came to me, whether or not they were motivated to change or were mandated to get therapy. I never wanted to be in a situation where I took on an unmotivated client because I had to pay my bills. I only work with clients that are eager and willing to get to work immediately and get quick results. My goal is always to do what's best for prospective clients and if I assess someone would be best served with another coach on my team with a different expertise or experience, I would recommend they worked with them instead of me.

Subsequent to getting my psychology degree, I went to business school and then got my coaching certifications. Now I'm helping people both in their businesses and personal lives. It keeps me very busy, but I love what I do!

Having Support

One thing I've always been really good at is choosing amazing people to be my friends. I surround myself with open-minded, non-judgmental people who genuinely want the best for others. I always make decisions on who I'll bring into my life based on how they make me feel. Do they make me laugh, are they happy for my success, do they make me feel good? When I leave them do I feel my inner joy has expanded? I really don't care about someone's age, colour, race or occupation, but if I feel someone is adding value to my life, they quickly become my friend.

I believe that no one is successful alone. Who you surround yourself with is critically important. I enjoy learning from others' experience and I prefer not to be the smartest person in the room, because then I learn more, I improve and make progress on my life's journey. Asking key questions and listening intently is essential to learning and whomever listens the most, learns the most.

I'm fortunate to have many beloved friends that are like my extended family and I've become a better business woman, parent and friend by having them in my life. They all accept me for who I am and are completely supportive of my goals. When I reach out to a friend for any type of support, I'm always humbled by the enthusiastic and spontaneous help I receive.

Going Through Tough Times

I developed my passion for skiing during a school trip to Switzerland when I was in grade 8 and decided when I was 16 that I wanted to move from mountainless Denmark where I was born and raised by parents who had never skied, so that I could ski all day and waitress at night to pay my bills. When I shared my plan with my mother she said, "If you want to be an empowered woman, I suggest you get educated." That made sense to me but I wanted to do both, so when I discovered Vancouver on an impromptu visit while touring North America, I fell in love with the city and the beauty of the mountain and ocean views.

I applied to the University of British Columbia and got accepted. When I told my parents I wanted to go to school in Vancouver, they thought it was ridiculous because education in Denmark is free, students get stipends, and money, and they have good cash flow. They said, "You want to move 8,000 km away, and pay three times the tuition as an international student? Why?" Well, to me it was simple, I wanted to be live in this beautiful city and explore all the ski resorts in the province! That was an expensive decision and came at a great sacrifice, but I certainly don't regret it and raising my family here has been a true privilege.

When I came to Vancouver from Copenhagen for my first year of university my boyfriend at the time was supportive and he flew back and forth from Europe to Vancouver to visit me. On my first Christmas break, I flew back to Europe, and had my "happy accident" when I became pregnant with my son. Overestimating the physical toll of having a baby, I thought I could still go back to school in September a few weeks after he was born and continue my studies. It took three days to give birth to him and I had to feed him every 3 hours. I felt as though I was going to die from a lack of sleep, so I decided that I might as well go back to Europe, have the family I wanted, and then come back and finish my degree.

When I was five months pregnant with my daughter, I was living in Amsterdam, and I wanted to move from a penthouse in the city to a house in the suburbs for more space for our expanding family, so my partner and I decided to move after Christmas to start the new year in our new home. I had planned the move and on moving day as I was standing on the street next to the moving van, I noticed that a lot of our furniture and belongings were missing. I called my partner and asked him about it. He told me not to worry and that he would get to the bottom of it. He showed up much later and he told me that he was going to stay in the apartment and that he was leaving us. To say that I was shocked and completely devastated would be a gross understatement. I didn't see it coming at all. I had no idea what to do next and what I would tell my children when they were old enough to ask.

Initially, money wasn't an issue as my ex-partner supported our children financially, but I learned very quickly that the real golden rule is whoever has the gold makes the rules, because as soon as I told my ex that I wanted to move back to Vancouver to finish my degree, I was cut off financially. I never saw a dime of child support and had to raise my children on my own. If my mother hadn't stepped in to help us financially, our lives would have been dramatically different with very limited educational opportunities.

I moved back to Vancouver when my daughter was 18 months old and my son was almost 3 years old. I had a full course load, I worked and did volunteer work at Birthright, counselling pregnant teenagers. I also provided education and support to people living with cancer and their families at the Canadian Cancer Society. Every minute of my day was scheduled and it was the most stress I've ever gone through in my life, emotionally and physically. The most stressful time was the year that I had all my finals in 3 days and my kids had chickenpox. Before that, I had been fortunate enough to have had at least a full study day in between exams to cram for the next exam. The fact that my kids had chickenpox meant they couldn't go to preschool, so I was with them 24/7 doing nursing duties, and trying to study. I went three or four days without sleep. I thought, *If I can get through this and survive, I think I can do anything.*

Overcoming Adversity

It took determination and a lot of patience over a ten year period to get through this. I had to find the courage to ask a lot of people for help that weren't family or friends. I would ask classmates to help me at certain times to pick my kids up from school. I lived in family housing on campus, and got to know my neighbours, and parents in the preschool, and I would ask if they could watch my children for 2 or 3 hours here and there to get some study time and in return I would babysit their kids. Every time I felt exhausted and on the verge of calling it quits, I would remind myself of my father telling me, "You can't take on a full course load at university and raise two kids all by yourself. You won't make it." Remembering that made me angry and determined enough to dig deep and find that extra energy to keep going. At other times, I would think, *I can't give up. I have these two people depending on me who didn't ask to be born and I love them more than life itself. I have to be successful.*

What Got Me Through

Pure passion and persistence got me through. I was very determined to create a life for my children that I felt they deserved. I had to stay focused and remind myself that they were totally dependent on me and that I had no option other than getting the education I needed to have a career that would allow me to provide for them. Having that focus and reminding myself of the end result every time I felt drained of energy, gave me just enough of a spark to continue. It was sheer grit and determination.

One very practical exercise that helped me enormously was a time management assignment I was given in Psychology 101. It effectively made you look at all the hours in a week as time blocks and decide how to use them. Being analytical that way, helped me allocate my study hours based on when my children were in day care, school or sleeping. Trying to do what I could to exhaust my daughter so she would fall asleep was a big challenge, especially on weekends. How do you exhaust a hyperactive 3-year old while conserving enough energy and motivation to get through studying for your biochemistry final once she finally falls asleep at 10:00 PM? She was high energy by nature and in preschool nap time was mandatory for all the children, so she would be super-energized when she got home. I practically begged the preschool staff not to allow her to nap in the afternoon, but of course the children's nap time is the only break the caregivers get, so that's not a battle I won. Time management became something I had to become very good at and I did.

I'm a big believer in nurturing your physical, mental, and spiritual health. Body, mind, and spirit are connected. You can work your physical body and maybe you look great, you're in shape, but your mind may be full of toxic beliefs that diminish your quality of your life and relationships. That's going to affect your body, as well as the food you eat.

Nutrition is fuel for your body and food is medicine; it can be toxic or it can be healing. And if you have long days, you need to have the right nutrition to sustain your energy and a lot of that has to do with sleep and food. Adding healthy, daily rituals into my life to address body, mind and soul helped and it's a continuous process. I'm open to trying anything new and staying with what works best for me.

I do believe in the power of silence and having moments of being in your bliss. For me, that happens when I ski or get engrossed in a great book. If you engage in an activity where time seems to evaporate, you're just in the moment enjoying it—I think that's nurturing for your mind, body, and soul.

My dad passed away from brain cancer very suddenly a year ago, and I decided that I must have joy in my life every day, something that is just pure fun. I decided being busy wasn't an excuse to not make the time. It doesn't have to be expensive or take a lot of time. It could be me dancing in my kitchen for 5 minutes to a current favourite song. I don't care what it is, it just needs to be something that's joyful. I love a good laugh which also happens to boost your immune system, reduce inflammation, and improve circulation, and my son helps me with that because he's a natural comedian and the funniest person I know. He has the unique ability to get me into a belly- aching laughter very quickly. Buddhism has the laughing Buddha to remind us of the healing nature of laughter. I wish it was a rule in every religion.

The Importance of Mindset

Mindset is everything because if you go around telling

yourself you can't, or you find excuses why you can't achieve something, you won't. What you tell yourself is essential and what you focus on will become your reality. There's power in the language you use when you speak to others and yourself, because the words you think will determine how you feel and if you don't feel good, you won't have the motivation or the energy to do what you need to do, to get where you want to be.

It's easy to tell ourselves a story focusing on the negative more than the facts. If we are going to tell ourselves stories, we might as well tell ourselves ones that will empower us and put us in a winning mindset. No matter what struggles come our way, we have the ability to process our emotions. I recommend writing about emotions in a journal because it allows you to get out of your head and separate yourself from the impact of the experience which in turns lets you choose how to respond to a situation with your rational mind instead of your emotions. It also temporarily breaks the cyclical pattern of reliving the same sad memories or depressing talk tracks. Replacing negative words with strong words will strengthen your emotions and mindset. For example, instead of telling yourself that you're "depressed' you could tell yourself you're "unstoppable" and "too strong to be knocked down permanently".

Find friends or family for emotional support to help drive your life forward. No one is ever successful alone and we will all face struggles in life but it's less difficult to weather storms knowing you have someone who will listen and offer a shoulder to cry on and a helping hand.

5 Tips to Overcoming Adversity

1. Make a decision to win.

2. Surround yourself with people who truly want you to succeed.

3. Ask for help.

4. Set your ego aside and ask for constructive feedback from high achievers that can be brutally honest with kindness.

5. Stay focused on the end result and take daily steps to reach your goal.

Someone told me once—and it always stuck with me—when you're thinking about adversity, about the hard things in life, remember that planes take off against the wind, not with it. Once you have a clear vision of what success means to you, find a right strategy, create an action plan, and never lose sight of the end goal until you achieve it. Relentless focus is mandatory.

For each challenge you overcome, you have added to your personal history of success or good choices. It's remarkably easy to forget about all the great decisions we've made and all our achievements and just think of poor outcomes or the negative consequences of potential decisions. Be your own cheerleader sometimes; review your history of accomplishments and give yourself a pat on the back. Your past successes are evidence that you've gone through hard times before and not only survived but became wiser and emotionally stronger. When you catch yourself in a negative cycle of thinking, just stop and recall 5 successes you've had. Keep a list of your personal and career achievements.

Sometimes I remind myself that despite not being a perfect parent or having perfect children, I accomplished my parenting objective. I raised two children, now adults, that are leaders not followers, that think for themselves, are financially literate, have chosen their own religions and most importantly act as members of the universe and not as if they are the centre of it. They're charitable, content adults always willing to help where it's needed. I think that's a huge accomplishment because parenting is the most important and toughest responsibility we take on.

An Important Lesson I Learned

If you want to go through life as the master of your own destiny, you can't rely on other people 100%. To be truly empowered, you have to be self-sufficient whether you're single or not. In order to build your emotional strength, you have to cultivate the belief that you can handle the challenges life throws at you. That doesn't mean you won't ever feel overwhelmed, unable to cope or weak, it means you have to build up enough confidence to say *Whatever comes my way, I'm emotionally equipped to handle it.* And you have to believe it.

There are a million excuses you make to give yourself permission to do something that you know isn't healthy for you, emotionally, physically, or socially. One rule of thumb I go by to get back on track whenever my inner child just wants to seek pleasure and forget about the consequences is to take a deep breath and remind myself that every decision I make in my life, big or small, is taking me one step towards my goal or not. So what do I want to do? Move forward or move back? There's no in-between. I try to get rid of the excuses that are so easy to make and focus on the results I want to achieve instead.

And sometimes it's just taking that deep breath, thinking about it, going for a walk, clearing your head. I try not to make any important decisions at the end of the day when I'm tired. I prefer to sleep on it, put it aside, and think about it during my peak time to increase the odds of it being a good decision. I get the facts on the table, try to take emotions out of it, talk to someone who gives me good advice and understands me well.

Another key lesson that I learned, is that you have to take responsibility for your own well-being and happiness. It's not someone else's responsibility to make or keep you happy. I spend time with people that inspire me and encourage me to find my joy. As much as my daughter's endless energy used to fatigue me when she was a toddler, today her joie de vivre and excitement in planning her next travel adventure is contagious. She's a constant reminder of not taking life too seriously and that squeezing every ounce of joy from every day is a thrilling, life-affirming habit.

About the Author

Pascale Hansen

Stellar Life Strategies
(778) 319-1825
www.stellarlifestrategies.com
Email: info@stellarlifestrategies.com
Facebook: Stellarlifestrategies
Twitter: @stellarlife5

As an international payments and foreign currency risk consultant at Western Union Business Solutions in Vancouver, Pascale Hansen helps companies improve cash flow, manage risk, and seize global market opportunities using customized currency risk management solutions. Pascale is also a life strategist and personal coach with Stellar Life Strategies and a financial architect with World Financial Group.

Chapter 8:

Move Forward – You Are a Better Person Because of Your Life Experience

By Adrienne Friedland Blumberg

Adrienne Friedland Blumberg is a Licensed Marriage and Family Therapist in San Diego. She is passionate about her work. She is loving, nurturing, caring, and understanding. Whether it is the adults she works with or their children, she always tries to walk in somebody else's shoes – she wants to feel how they feel and understand what they are going through. She is a thoughtful and loyal friend, who is always there when she's needed.

Being a Marriage and Family Therapist

As a licensed Marriage and Family Therapist I have come full circle in my own being. I always had a strong sense of self and a powerful personality, with an incredibly gentle soul. My passion for understanding others is tremendous as I have the unique ability to fine tune my listening skills and zero in on issues that present themselves within the therapy room.

I know my clients are ever so grateful for their experiences that they have navigated through. It's tough and not an easy feat. Others see me as a committed professional who extends herself whenever possible. As I state to my clients, "I am a text message away." However, with this said, I do create boundaries inside and outside the therapy room. I must practice what I preach.

My profession is one that requires a person to be honorable, trustworthy and committed. If one fulfills these three characteristics, it's a recipe for success. My profession is very humbling and a gift if you are excellent at what you do. When I hear, "It will take you several sessions to get through to my child" or "I've been in therapy before and it didn't help" or "It's worth a try because I have nothing to lose" - it challenges me to work harder. I look for a small opening that I can maneuver my way through, allowing me to engage in a way that is calming, soothing, compassionate and intriguing. I know my clients have told me I just get it, I am so understanding and it's as if "you have walked in my shoes."

We all have problems. The grass is never greener on the other side. Individuals who come into therapy ranging in age from 5 to 95 are there for a reason. With the youngest clients, the parents feel their child needs extra help, however it's really the parents that need guidance in order to help their child. Problems are in the eyes of the beholder. One's problem is another's solution. Working on behaviors, parenting, anger, self-esteem, divorce, blended families, infidelity, and anxiety pertaining to life in general are critical to those who walk past my threshold. Nothing is impossible when one has hope, connection, goals, commitment, honesty and trust. It goes both ways with the therapist and the client.

Why I Do What I Do

As a professional I believe that one must have passion for what one does. If one lacks zest for one's work, it is brutally painful to get your act together and muster up the energy to get there on a daily basis. I am so fortunate that my profession is nourishing for the soul and the energy in the therapy room is nothing but positive.

I am a mother, a wife, a mentor and everything in between. As a seasoned professional adult who has walked through and dealt with many life experiences, I have grown into the adult that I hoped I would be.

My upbringing, as a child of Holocaust survivors, has shaped me into who I am today. My parents were survivors: one survived the concentration camp Theresienstadt, and the other survived the war in Uzbekistan. Coming from a family of survivors instilled in me the belief that I can do what I want; I was raised to understand the importance of having to stand on your own two feet as nothing in life is guaranteed. My parents instilled good strong moral values while growing up. As my parents said, "Be a Mensch" which is the Yiddish word for having integrity and honor. I carried this through the ebbs and flows of my life to my advantage and also to my detriment, as you will read about later.

My life experiences have not all been positive yet only good things have happened from my not so good experiences. Rabbi Harold S. Kushner's book *When Bad Things Happen to Good People* explains this concept well. I asked myself that after I was faced with adversity in my life. I strive to be the best person that I can be, filled with love and compassion and this has been my gift that has carried me through the last 60 years of my life.

My Early Career

I always knew that I would work with people; in what capacity I wasn't sure. I grew up in the small city of Windsor, in southwestern Ontario, Canada. Growing up, my mother called me "Mother Goose." Whenever there was an issue with my friends and their friends I would find them at my doorstep for a lot of TLC to help them get through their crisis. This started in middle school and lasted all through high school and university.

I secured my first job as a cashier at K-Mart at the age of 16 and then worked as a pharmacy assistant until I left for university. I was always mindful of the importance of standing on my own two feet and being independent. I worked as a camp counselor, I worked with children and I volunteered in the Psychiatric ward of Women's Hospital in Toronto while attending university. Then I became a unit head at a day camp in Toronto and later worked as a counselor at overnight camp in Quyon, Quebec.

My path always led me to work with people. After graduating university and college in Canada, I pursued a job as a teacher at the Mandelcorn Center, a prestigious private school helping children with learning differences and behavior issues. Remembering the importance of standing on my own two feet, two years later I opened my own private facility, with a partner, in the affluent Forest Hill area of Toronto.

I married at 28 years of age, which was old for that time, believe it or not. I had no regrets, just more life experience under my belt. My husband was attracted to my "entrepreneurial spirit" as he mentioned in his wedding speech to me. We had two boys, Sam and Myles, who kept me incredibly busy in addition to my work. Not only did I have the learning center, I opened an art center for children as well. I needed to keep going, to make the best of my life that I could. Values and beliefs are so important - they can mold you and change you as you navigate through life.

After working as a teacher/tutor for 13 years, my husband and I decided that the winters were too cold in Toronto and we were looking to move to a warmer climate, which translated to moving out of Canada. We looked at Arizona, Florida and California. California was the best choice for our family at that time. So the immigration process started. It was a grueling 18 month process. It separated my husband and I for nearly 12 months. He needed to make sure that the move would be viable before schlepping the entire family 3200 miles away. The common thread being woven through my life story is that of survival, competence, dedication, commitment, goals and connection.

Arriving in the United States in the summer of 1993, I was in a new home, yet it felt like being on vacation. No friends or family to be found anywhere, but I had no regrets. My eldest son struggled for a year, at age 6; he missed his friends and had trouble adjusting to his new environment. I was not able to work as my papers did not come through yet so I thoroughly enjoyed being with my children. It was an awesome and soul nourishing experience because I had always been a working mom since they were born.

I eventually went back to tutoring and was hired by one of the school districts as an instructional aide, where I worked for 5 years. I loved the camaraderie, the families, the children and my colleagues. I worked in all classes from kindergarten through 6th grade. I still have wonderful memories of that time.

Facing a Very Difficult Challenge

In 2000, I was contacted by a head hunter, who asked if I would be interested in working as a Director in Early Childhood for a non-profit. That sounded great; it was right up my alley and I could utilize my early childhood education to promote the importance of this field and profession. After several interviews, I was hired and I started my job in the summer of 2000. I was excited to put my passion to work.

Being from back east, work ethics and expectations were a little different than the laid back Californian culture. I was from the era of got it—do it—get it done. No pussy footing around for days until you felt like it. It was a challenge for me to hold my staff up to my standards. With that said, my family's value system kept kicking in.

My job was exhilarating, fulfilling and I loved it. I minded my own business and took care of my department as best as I could. I had high expectations of my staff and most knew what my expectations were. Being the head of a department, I was managing 25 plus staff members and ultimately the final decision came from me, most of the time. Life was good. I was praised for the outstanding job I was doing, stellar reviews and one individual even told me, "You walk on water." The department raised a great deal of money allowing us to embellish and grow our program and sit comfy. Every day was a blessing. Notwithstanding that every job has its ebbs and flows but nothing like what happened to me.

I have to take a deep breath as my sanctuary began to crumble. I trusted my staff, loved each and every one of them for who they were yet all that I gave was taken and I received nothing in return. Control, dishonesty, backstabbing and trust had all been violated. As I tried to nurture my profession and make it a representation of who I was, I was slashed at the knees. I will never forget the day.

The prior couple of months, my gut was telling me that something was not right. I felt it. I trusted it. I reached out to others and no one uttered a word. I didn't know what it was but I knew something was "off."

I knew that I could not advance higher in this system, so I decided to go back to graduate school, to obtain my Masters in Marriage and Family Therapy. This to me made the most sense as I saw it as an extension of my job. Parents would make appointments to see me, thinking they would want to discuss their child in my program. However, it was anything but that; they talked about themselves, their other kids, their spouses. I knew I needed to pursue the next level of my life. I did not know what was waiting for me on the horizon. I believed I would graduate in 8 years, work and be in my happy place.

My Happy Place Became a Nightmare

It was June 14th, 2007. I'll never forget it. A day or two before, my supervisor scheduled a meeting with me at 5:00 in the afternoon. And I walked into the room, I saw my supervisor and four other board members sitting there. I asked, "Why am I here?" I had a gut feeling. My gut is excellent. This wasn't going to be a little coffee chat or pulling out a bottle of cognac to cheer on something. I sat down. I remember one woman on the board saying to me, "This has been very difficult, but it's a decision we made. You have lost the vision of what we're all about and things have come across our way and we have to let you go," and the other one just handed me a paycheck. Their reasoning was I had lost vision of what this institution stood for. My vision was not the same as theirs.

My vision wasn't lost. California is an "at will" state. Legally, they don't have to give you any reason when letting you go from a job. I was never written up in 7 years for doing something wrong. I would have meetings with my supervisor every week; I met with a parent every month because she was the liaison for my department to the other building and she would always say to me, "Everything is so great, everybody is so happy, everybody loves what you're doing," and then suddenly out of the blue I am fired one day.

It felt like I got hit by a Mack truck. I was bowled over. I didn't even hear what they were saying in the sense that I couldn't believe what I was hearing. So I turned and looked at the President of the Board, and I said to him, "Didn't we just have a meeting two days ago? And I talked about concerns that I had, and you told me not to worry, that everything was going to be great, and you would take it over and take it up with whoever it needed to be taken up with? Now you're sitting here and this is what you're doing to me?" He couldn't look me straight in the face. Actually, none of them could. This was the worst thing that I have ever imagined would happen to someone who was strong, dedicated, passionate, nurturing, loving, and hard-working.

How I Felt

I felt horrible, humiliated, disrespected. How could someone do this to another human being? How could somebody in this non-profit organization, who deals with individuals who have all different kinds of needs, do this? This was a religious organization who preached kindness and respect, and they did not practice what they preached, especially my narcissistic supervisor. They basically stabbed me in the back, took what I could give them, and let me go.

It took me a good two to three years to get over that. It felt like I had PTSD driving near the facility because that was a road that I travelled on—I couldn't avoid going in that direction. I had to re-live this horrible situation. Having to go home and tell my husband I was just let go. I don't think he heard what I said because it didn't make any sense. But it did make sense after I pieced everything together. How my supervisor needed control, and always hired divorced women who were vulnerable and needed jobs. That's who he surrounded himself with. I wasn't in that building. And no one would talk to me, no one would give any explanation to me. It was like I was a leper. No one would return telephone calls, no one wanted to have anything to do with me, for fear their jobs would be on the line. Except one person did, who was very high up on the command chain. They said to her, "If you breathe a word, if you give Adrienne any heads up this is happening, you will lose your job." So what does a single woman do?

Overcoming This Situation

It took me about 2 years to get over this blow. I did it through therapy. I was in therapy because I was embarking on my new profession, which was already in the works, and I felt that this was a good time to really experience what therapy was all about. I was in intense therapy for 2 years trying to make sense of what happened. Eventually I did make sense of what happened and could therefore let it go and now I look at all of them and I have pity for them. I pity that people have to go to extremes like that, and can really put their heads down at night and sleep, when not only have they destroyed my income, but not taking into account that I had two kids, one of which was already in college, and there was a mortgage to be paid, and bills to be paid. And we had created a lifestyle based on our two incomes and we were stripped of that.

Do I wish I still worked there? No. I think that had to happen in order for me to do the best work that I could do with people. They say one door closes and another one opens, and we are put in places for a reason, and I think I needed to experience that in order to take me to the next level and become the therapist that I am. That is compassion, that is understanding, really being able to step into someone else's shoes. And the interesting thing, you know who my first client was? A 45-year-old woman, who worked for a church, who was let go for no reason. Things happen in mysterious ways. I was able to help her understand and empower her that it wasn't her fault, to move forward and just put one foot in front of the other.

Sometimes when you're in the middle of it, you don't see the rainbow, you don't see the light at the end of the tunnel. It was almost like I felt embarrassed for the organization that I worked for. I still do feel embarrassed for the organization I worked for. And the next year, it was another woman this happened to, and just last year, another woman.

Developing The Right Mindset

It is incredibly important to think positively. You have to think the best, and that there is a reason for what has happened and your cup is not half empty, it's not half full— it's continuing to replenish itself, which means the mindset always has to be there to keep moving you forward. If you let yourself get dragged down and you go down that dark hole again, it just doesn't work.

What Worked For Me

My best therapy was talk therapy. I needed to piece things together to make sense of my world and have someone there to validate and be brutally honest with me. Was I healthy minded? I exercised a lot, did yoga, took walks. I needed to get myself healthy, mind-wise. And immersing myself into school was a blessing because I was already enrolled into my program prior to this starting and I already had a class under my belt. This just expedited it and made it happen quicker.

I would tell any woman that if you have a healthy mindset, you can accomplish anything you want. It's when you're stuck in your own thoughts and the mindset becomes toxic and unhealthy, you're no good to anyone.

Life is beautiful and I knew and believed in myself, given my roots, my foundation, my belief system and my support system. Friends are friends but your true friends will be there though life's challenges and good times. I learned that I have no use for fair-weather friends. My life is too important to me and I want to fill it with those that are special, loving and meaningful.

I grew into an even stronger person than before. I didn't think it possible but life is always full of surprises, and yes, my gut served me well and people who entered my life at that point in time proved me correct in believing there was nothing wrong with me but the system was broken.

I have learned that honesty, trust and compassion are necessities in life. I have learned that surrounding yourself with good people that are respectful, honest, loving and caring is the best gift you can give to yourself.

3 Tips On How to Choose Success Over Adversity

1. Believe in yourself. Know in your heart who you are. Those that try to diminish are diminished themselves.

2. Be able to dodge something thrown at you and then keep going.

3. Success is the biggest pat on the back you can give yourself. By being successful, it comes with so many accolades and so many rewards personally, as what you can impart on those lives you touch, those people you come into contact with. Because they feel it. I'm smiling all the time. I'm just a happy person. I'm very rarely down and depressed. I'm always in good spirits. I think by being able to uplift yourself, that is the gift that you have to touch the lives of other women that are not as fortunate or blessed as you.

When Going Through a Challenging Time

It's important to have a strong support system, to believe in yourself, and remember that there's nothing in life you cannot accomplish if you're passionate about it.

I want to thank my phenomenal therapist, Debra Moceri who helped me through the darkest part of my life and thank my family who is a source of my strength. Being hard working, believing, dedicated, compassionate, and loving, has helped mold me into the woman I am today. Under no circumstances will I allow this to happen again and will support my clientele on all levels helping them find their internal resources and moving them to external resources that can strengthen the very person they believe they can be.

About the Author

Adrienne Friedland Blumberg

Adrienne Blumberg, MA MFT RPT
Approved supervisor
858-349-1422
760-729-5900
www.adrienneblumbergtherapy.com

Adrienne is a Licensed Marriage and Family Therapist with a Masters Degree from Alliant International University, San Diego. She has been working with children, teens, adults and families for over 30 years and her career experience spans from being a parent and educator to a coach/mentor for professionals, fellow students and parents. She counsels children, families, individuals and couples on all issues impacting one's healthy and productive life-style. As a skilled professional in the field of psychotherapy and an experienced educator, she is a compassionate and creative individual who demonstrates high standards and ethics foremost in counseling, mentoring and coaching, thus providing a creative, safe environment in which her clients can develop and re-discover the "self" that they want to be.

Over the last 4 years she has been a member of The American Association for Marriage and Family Therapist (AAMFT) in addition to a member of the California Association of Marriage and Family Therapists (CAMFT). She is also a Registered Play Therapist and proudly holds membership in the Association of Play Therapy. Adrienne is the proud mother of 2 grown children and she has been married for 31 years.

Chapter 9:

Change Doesn't Happen Overnight

By Lynn Williams

Lynn Williams owns The Lifestyle Protector, a boutique professional financial advice company that works with business owners, entrepreneurs, lawyers and other professionals to help them do more with their money. Lynn is both capable and caring. She has a beautiful combination of skill and compassion that helps people feel they're in good hands. Clients can ask any question without fearing their question is stupid. Lynn's compassion is rooted a personal and professional journey that leveraged adversity.

How We Help People

At **The Lifestyle Protector** we help people make decisions about their money. We pull all the pieces of their financial puzzle together to look at their big financial picture. We help them set priorities and take action to help them move from where they are today to where they want to be. We focus on helping clients build confidence and on empowering them to make better financial decisions. We also help clients prepare positively for their retirement.

While I have a professional background in accounting, that's not the only reason I'm able to help people with their money. I didn't start out knowing what I was doing with my own money, and I certainly didn't start out knowing how to grow a business built on helping others financially. Getting to where I am was difficult and full of adversity. I've been on my own journey with money, and this has provided me with both the skill and the compassion that I bring to the caring work we do at **The Lifestyle Protector**.

How I Got Started In This Industry

My Dad started this business in the 1960s. I was a chartered accountant and had been working and living in Australia and New Zealand for 22 years. About a year after my Dad was diagnosed with cancer, in 2008, he said to me, "Why don't you come back to Canada and put your chartered accountancy skills to work in my business? Why not come back and work for me?" I knew my Dad wasn't well. I had already been thinking that I would like to come home and spend more time with him because we didn't know how long he had left.

I knew what was involved with being an employee, and I was a good one. I came back to Canada, expecting to become my dad's employee, just like he said. But when I got here, my Dad was grateful I was here, his illness had progressed, and his priorities had shifted and changed. It was almost as though he said, "Great, you're here, I'm done. It's all yours, go for it."

I didn't know if I could do it. I hadn't envisioned myself as a business owner and hadn't expected to take over as leader immediately. I thought there would be some sort of window that I could learn the industry and get up to speed. I was hoping to have a little bit of a runway to learn and slowly take over. Instead, it was a hard start. Very hard.

I found myself left to figure it all out on my own. I hadn't lived in Canada for 22 years, so it felt like I was in a new country. And I was in a new city, where I knew no one. My dad was based in Victoria but he insisted that I should be in Vancouver because it was a bigger centre. He believed I would be able to grow the business more from Vancouver. I was in a new industry, too. I hadn't ever worked in the financial planning industry and knew very little about financial advice.

My family was in Victoria and my dad wasn't well. I was faced with all these new challenges and I didn't know how to help people in the ways my father did. Could I help people even if I didn't have the experience?

My shift from employee to entrepreneur was like being dropped into this deep black crevice. All I could think was where do I go, what do I do?

There were a lot of tears in those first two to three years. I cried a lot.

But I did it. And in the years since, I've accomplished two significant things:

- Built a comprehensive financial planning business (my dad mainly focused on life insurance), and

- More than tripled the amount of financial assets we manage for clients.

What Drives Me To Do What I Do

What drives me has shifted over the years I've been at the helm of **The Lifestyle Protector**. In the early days, it was my dad's legacy. It was really, really important to me not to mess it up. I was driven to continue his legacy, to continue to serve his clients as well as I possibly could because his clients were really important to him. He cared about them and I wanted to make sure that I was respecting that, protecting that, and by extension protecting his legacy.

What drives me today is my passion for empowering people. I thrive on helping them build their confidence around managing money and decisions around money, particularly when it's not something they are comfortable with. Some people are happy talking about and making decisions around money. But most of us are not. Even though we know it's important and even though we know we need to think about it and do something about it, for many of us money talk feels like a foreign language.

The terminology is specific, and it can be confusing to figure out why choose this product over that. What drives me today is my passion for helping make this opaque world of finance clear for people so they can make better financial decisions and plan for the future – based on what's important to them.

How Others Reacted When I Took Over The Business

My immediate family were very supportive and my Dad was very, very grateful. He believed I was capable because of my chartered accountancy and corporate background. My closest friends wondered what the heck I was doing.

My dad, bless his soul, was never really a mentor for me or my sisters. It just didn't come naturally to him that he would pass on his financial and business wisdom. I would call him to ask, "What would you do in this situation?" And he would say, "It's your decision now. You have to live with the decision. You make the decision."

His attitude was always: You figure it out. I would think, *I'm actually calling you because of your experience in the industry, your experience with dealing with these things. I truly want to know how you would have dealt with it. I'm just calling for some advice.* Once in a while he might give me his opinion, but then he would say, "But you still decide what you want to do." That was the extent of his mentorship. I certainly couldn't rely on it to get me out of a pinch.

Dad's confidence in me was both a blessing and a curse: he was confident I would find my own way, and I did. But it was at a significant cost. It was one of the hardest periods of my life.

I'm really fortunate I have some very, very good friends from Australia and New Zealand and in the first couple of years I had a steady stream of friends visiting me. They said, "My goodness what have done? You've made this huge change!" I was very lucky that I had friends that would make the trip and take the time to come and see me and meet me where I was at in my stress and craziness. They provided moral support, but I felt very much on my own for business support.

Dealing With Adversity

I was stressed all the time. When I look back, I see what I call a front stage and a backstage. In the front stage, I was continually trying to present that everything was okay and functioning. I was trying to present that I was a success and that I knew exactly what I was doing.

Backstage is where it was real. I worked extremely long hours. I was up at seven and was still working at 1:00 a.m. I was trying to figure out all the pieces of this brand new complex puzzle. I didn't do any socializing other than work, networking and work-related activities. I didn't take any holidays. I worked all weekend every weekend. It was a constant drive and a single-minded focus, with a constant underlying stress. I wasn't calm backstage at all. I was stressed and I'm sure that came through even though I tried to keep the front stage looking like everything was under control. The backstage stress dominated everything. There was an overwhelming fear that was always present. It almost broke me down.

While all this was going on, my Dad was unwell. The Canadian Cancer Society was fantastic as a support too. They offered counseling to our family through the grief process, which I took advantage of. It really helped me understand my own feelings about what was happening with my father, and how that blended into the feelings I had around this new business and the responsibility on my shoulders.

Overcoming Adversity

It wasn't long before I realized I could, in fact, do this. I found that I was comfortable talking numbers and money in a way that not everyone is – even other financial professionals. So that was the biggest thing that helped me deal with the adversity: a recognition I was capable of this after all. Self-belief.

Once that set in, it helped me gain the confidence to seek help where I was weak. When I was an employee in large corporations, I never had to worry about business development, or the sales process. And that meant I really didn't know how to approach these key areas of my new business.

Business development was my biggest stumbling block and my biggest fear. How do I go to market? How do I talk to people about this? How am I going to find clients? I think the key thing was getting help from a business development coach who could really help me understand that whole process and help me not take it so personally.

I came up with an analogy around relationships and dating that really helped. When you go on your first date you do not expect a marriage proposal. When I go to my first meeting with a prospective new client, I'm not going to expect to sign a contract. I learned to become really comfortable getting to know someone, sharing my knowledge and helping people with where they are at. I also learned to ask, "Where are you at in your situation?" and to be okay with the response.

Change didn't happen overnight. It took about three years. That was long enough to see that this thing hadn't fallen over and I've been able to maintain and grow the business. I started to believe that I can help people. I saw how I was helping people and that momentum started to build for me, which was fantastic.

Overcoming adversity is an ongoing process. There's a Richard Branson quote that says, "There are no quick wins in business. It takes years to become an overnight success." When I'm talking to other entrepreneurs and business owners, they've shared that they start to feel the business gets a lot easier in that seven to ten years, not in that first five years. I'd agree with that.

Another key way I overcame the adversity of those first few years was to begin to think about the business as an entity separate from me. I think of it as a child. In the first five years children need a lot more support, and a lot more guidance. You can barely put the child down.

It's the same with my business. In the first few years I couldn't let my guard down: I had to make sure it was fed and watered and had enough sleep. The right attention to the right things matters. I often think about the business in this way: what stage of development is a person at when it is five years old, ten years old, even fifteen? A ten-year-old has her own personality and stronger sense of identity than a five-year-old. A fifteen-year-old business is still just a teenager, complete with hormonal swings and emotional meltdowns.

Holding onto my *Why* has really helped me. Remembering why am I doing this: part legacy of my Father and part my own drive to empower people around their finances. That was a real anchor point for me. I think if people are starting a business and they don't have a strong *Why*, the hardship or the challenges can become so overwhelming that they want to quit. Holding onto my *Why* kept me going.

The other thing that I do annually is take a meditation retreat. I hand my phone to my assistant and she clears all my emails. I let people know that I'm not going to be available. That ten-day letting-go period really helps me to refocus and recentre. I have found that yoga is also a big part of feeling centred during the day-to-day craziness.

I'm a big walker and I make good use of the motivation of my Fitbit. I find walking is a really great way to facilitate thinking. If I have a problem, I'm amazed how my thoughts start to get clearer and an idea comes to mind about how I might solve that problem during a short 20-25-minute walk.

Your Mindset is Important

It's important not to ignore your feelings. It's important to acknowledge when you feel scared, nervous, and uptight. It's about what action you will take with the feeling, because I really do believe that action moves us forward. Sometimes it seems like our society is not okay with people feeling down or being frustrated or angry or concerned or worried. I think it is important to be okay with sitting in worry for a while and say, "This is what worry feels like. Now what action will I take in order to help me feel less worried?" Sitting and worrying isn't going to solve my problem, but at least I'm acknowledging my worry rather than ignoring it or pushing it down. I believe that what you resist persists. It's important not to resist those feelings but to acknowledge them, figure how you want to do to move forward, and then move through those feelings.

Sometimes the universe might say, "Not that path. That's not necessarily the right action." Then you have to re-group.

How I Have Changed

I'm an entirely different person now than I was when I started this journey. How has it made me stronger? I no longer have fear running constantly through me. It's not that I don't become afraid of certain things or that I don't fear certain situations. But I don't go through life in such a constant state of fear. I embrace life and what it has to offer a lot more easily.

I've also learned that I'm really my own biggest limitation. I try to concentrate on what I really want in life and how I want to live my life. As an employee, so much of what I did in my life was based on what somebody else wanted me to do. Then when I became a self-employed entrepreneur, it took time for me to realize I could create my own world. That has made me a different person. I'm a stronger person now and I can say, "This is what I want to contribute and this is how I want to do it."

Important Skills

I learned a lot about visualizing what I want and setting goals to achieve it. Those skills are cornerstones to my day-to-day now. Now I use visualization to determine what I want in my life, what and who I want to be, and what I want my business to look like.

Being in business means you always have goals and projects on the go. But at a personal level it's becoming more and more important for me to visualize the life and the contribution I want to make. I didn't have that skill well-developed before. That's been a really important change for me that has really helped.

7 Tips to Choosing Success Over Adversity

1. Seek help. Figure out where you need help and find the help you need in order to address your challenge. There is no need to struggle alone.

2. People. You've got to have people around you that care about you. You may not even talk about the business or your adversity with them but it's important to have people that you can be yourself with. Have people around you that believe in you. Leave the ones aside that don't. They're for someone else.

3. Belief. Self-belief is a fundamental cornerstone. You know yourself better than anybody else. If you believe you will overcome, you will overcome. It may not be today or tomorrow. It may take a while, like it did with me, two or three or four years down the track. I really do believe that self-belief is a cornerstone of overcoming adversity.

4. Perseverance. You have to persist because adversity can be a very long road. One of my clients shared their practice around grief: when they lose a loved one they acknowledge that grief at one month, six months, nine months, one year and three years. That approach really does acknowledge that our grief process evolves

over a fairly long time. Perseverance is required to move through the often long life of adversity.

5. Take control. Take control of your situation and your circumstances as best you can by taking action that is best for you because you know yourself best.

6. Flexibility. Be open to flexibility, open to change. If you're on a track and nothing's working, sometimes you have to change tracks. You might think this is the way to do it but then have to find a different way. It's okay to make changes in the face of new information or a new experience.

7. Kindness. Be kind to yourself. It can be tough going through adversity and we're often our own worst critics. Whether being kind to yourself means taking a hot bath, or modifying negative self-talk, do be kind. All the support and kindness from others will mean nothing if you can't be kind to yourself.

I'm grateful that I've now come out the other side of adversity, and that I've been able to keep making my father's clients happy as well as build my business with new clients. Just the other day, I received this thank-you note from clients that were originally my father's, and are now mine:

"I'm thankful that I called you for advice. We think back at how lucky we all were to have met and got to know your Father, such a nice person. He helped us out so very much! Now we appreciate your help. Thank You!"

And it was all worth it.

About the Author

Lynn Williams

The Lifestyle Protector
www.lifestyleprotector.ca
Facebook: /TheLifestyleProtector
LinkedIn: /lynnwilliams2
Twitter: /LifestylePro

Lynn@LifestyleProtector.ca
Phone: 604 833 0348

http://lynnwilliams.me

Lynn Williams is a successful financial professional, marketer, business owner and CEO. As a professional financial advisor and president of The Lifestyle Protector, Lynn is motivated to see business owners and professionals do more with their money.

Lynn brings the skills, experience and expertise from chartered accounting and relationship marketing together in a personable and professional approach.

She enjoys nurturing financial confidence so clients take measurable steps towards meeting their aims and aspirations.

Chapter 10:

Don't Give Up When It Gets Hard!

By Kim Roy

Kim Roy is a family coach who works with families to empower them. As they go through difficult circumstances, she brings awareness that they are not alone and that they can have a 100% chance of having a healthy and happy marriage with the help of their Heavenly Father. She is especially sensitive to the needs and challenges facing blended families, since she and her husband are a blended family.

Divorce is all too common in this day and time. Just having someone who has been where you are makes such a difference. It gives you hope and a feeling that you will make it through.

Why I Became a Family Coach and What Drives Me to Do What I Do

Simply put, because I never believed for one minute that everything that happened to us was not meant to be a gift for someone else. I constantly said as we worked through each thing, there is a reason we are going through this. This is so painful, it *can't* just be for us. I know we are meant to share and lift the burdens of others in this life. And I felt so many impressions that this was one of the ways Heavenly Father intended for us to help.

Also, I have always tended to be the kind of person who learns from others' mistakes so I could avoid the unwanted pain. I learned to look at what we were going through as gifts, as strange as that sounds. One of my favorite quotes is: ***Things don't happen to me, things happen for me.*** I believe that we can find a gift in everything we go through if we search deeply enough.

One of the blessings of having gone through our difficult circumstances was that we became certified as marriage coaches, to teach Marriage on the Rock. Meaning Jesus.

Also having worked as a massage therapist years ago I was led into EFT - Emotional Freedom Technique – and having worked extensively with Karol Truman's book, *Feelings Buried Alive Never Die* over the last 12 years I have found that when we don't process trauma and negative feelings those become buried in the body. They have to go somewhere and that seemed to be much of why people would visit me as a massage therapist. I have taken my belief in Heavenly Father and my knowledge of the emotions, therapeutic grade essential oils, and my gift of journaling and combined them to help others. I absolutely believe if these things hadn't been present for us to access we would not be married today. I am so grateful for the gifts and talents Heavenly Father blessed me with. And I love seeing people overcome difficult circumstances and come out the victor.

When I Became a Family Coach

It came to me, really. I kept running into people that needed help in their marriage and honestly I kept trying to go another path. But it kept pulling me back. I knew in my heart that Heavenly Father wanted me to help others, but I held back for a time. I started out working on people with the emotional release work but kept getting the impression that my place was to work with couples.

My friends and family were very supportive when I decided to become a coach. Although one of my daughters said, "You're leaving massage therapy where you have a good job and you're established?" But the oldest said to me she felt it was inspired for us to take what we had learned and develop that into a way for helping others. Just working with our kids at first who were having challenges and teaching them what we had learned gave me the idea that it could be extremely helpful for others.

A terrible fall

I see wisdom as I look back at this part of my life. One of the consequences of divorce was a feeling of anger and alienation from the kids in those first years, especially with my youngest daughter. She was involved with 4-H and FFA (Future Farmers of America) because she loved animals and found solace in working with them. She also entered baked goods into the competitions. The enjoyment she received through sharing her baking with others was a great blessing for her. It was like therapy.

About a year and a half after we married and through all the turmoil we had been through I decided I had made a terrible mistake getting married again. I was fixing to take CEU classes to keep my massage therapy license current, thinking I would just move on, with much reservation. Neither Al nor I had any idea what we would face in dealing with the baggage we brought with us from our first marriage and also trying to adjust to each other and our new life. It was just too much.

Within the week after thinking that, I went to the fairgrounds one morning and was really excited to watch my daughter show her cow. Between shows she suggested we go sit on the bleachers. Little did I know she meant all the way to the top! There were no handrails so I was watching my footing so as not to fall. I kept looking down and out of my peripheral vision I could see that she had stopped and turned around, so I knew I should look up. When I looked up, the next thing I knew I hit my head on an unmarked beam and I fell backwards down four or five flights of seating landing mainly on the left side of my back. To this day I believe if I hadn't been knocked out for those few seconds I may have flailed and broken my neck or worse. As it was, I was left with a broken wrist in two places and reinjured my left meniscus in my knee and hurt my shoulder. We were so concentrated on the upper part of my body I didn't even know for about 8 weeks my knee was reinjured, because of the medication I was on for my wrist.

So the plan to take those classes was null and void because of the fall and my life was filled with healing of all kinds for the next two years. I went through physical therapy and three surgeries. I worked on me with counselors and Al and I went to two different marriage counselors together. And I learned at that point about EFT - Emotional Freedom Technique. Heavenly Father knew what I needed. I had many wounds that needed to be healed and they would never have been healed had I run away. I feel things would have gotten worse for me if had done that and I may not have been able to overcome the weaknesses that were affecting my marriage to Al or to anyone.

I had always wanted to help families. I just never knew I had so much work to be done on myself before I could even consider it as a possibility. After Al and I had gotten through the biggest part of our healing, I started pondering about working with families again instead of massage therapy. I had felt Heavenly Father's promptings to consider it and let go of the massage therapy. This was just the encouragement I needed.

As I was healing at home, I had plenty of time to research help for blended families and I found a website called Successful Stepfamilies and Marriage Today with Jimmy Evans and his wife.

These things were of great help to Al and I. We learned how to incorporate the things I had learned about the emotions and the essential oils into our healing and believe me, we spent lots of time holding each other's hands and praying because the last thing we needed or wanted was to go through a second divorce.

I just needed the encouragement to stay and work through it. And when Al said, "Kim, I am in this for the long haul," that changed things for me big time.

It told me he was committed to working things through no matter what. And once I knew where his head was, I recommitted also.

One day while I was alone in my apartment I was trying to do the laundry so my husband wouldn't have that to do when he got home. My arm being in a cast made it hard for me to do simple tasks in those first few weeks after the fall. I dragged the laundry basket in front of the dryer to pull the clothes into it. As I knelt down a bit, my left knee started hurting really bad and that is when I knew I had reinjured it. I had to reach far into the dryer to get the laundry and I had to take a few stabs at that. I started to cry. I was saying out loud to Heavenly Father, "I can't do this!" Meaning I can't get the laundry out. Then the tears came harder and the voice got louder. "I can't do this!" And then my heart just opened up and I really started crying with the realization of what I really meant, which was, "I can't do this pain anymore!" The pain of the surgeries, of being lonely in that apartment for months and the divorce from my first husband and the feeling of failure, all the pain from the problems in the second marriage was just too much to bear. Issues we had to work through that seemed to have no answers and that were ongoing and then the concern we had for the challenges our adult kids were facing in their lives. There were just so many things and the stress was always there. My spirit was just so exhausted and drained. Then I heard this....***Don't give up when it gets hard!*** It stopped me in my tracks and I thought about it. At first I applied it to the tasks around the house and then I applied it to life and our situation. It seemed to penetrate every part of me. It was a spiritual message from Heavenly Father just to me. I had a dream that let me know if I hung in there things would work out. It was so clear and real and very impressive. He knew what we were going through. He knew how I felt even when I didn't. The teacher is quiet while we are going through the test. When I wanted to give up, I remembered what I got that day and I would say, "Ok, deep breath..... breathe!" I am so happy we stayed with it because it has been worth the effort. But at the time, I couldn't see it.

Don't Give Up When It Gets Hard

Here are a few of the things that made our situation so difficult. I have so much more in my journals. You can't have an adequate picture in one chapter. What I share today is the tip of the iceberg compared to what we actually went through, but it will give you some idea.

The first couple of months were wonderful until the phone calls started from the ex-wife demanding things. He was spending two evenings a week with his kids away from me. I felt he needed to spend time with his boys but then the demands became greater in the area of time and finances. She wanted more of his time for relief for her with the kids. He had church callings down here with me during the week and because of her demands he couldn't even do his church calling. I believe she still wanted the wife status and with him being more of a passive type man it really created more issues for us to deal with! I finally told Al if she didn't back off I was going to make an appointment and visit her Bishop and let him know what was happening. It was not right. Instead I visited with Heavenly Father one night when I was so frustrated and recounted the story to him and the way I was feeling and after that I have to say things calmed down dramatically! And all was quiet for a good long while. We did go visit our Bishop where I got a blessing and we got some good counsel from him. We also started seeing a marriage counselor shortly after that because if we were to overcome these things we needed more help than we had. Then we were dealing with triggers and baggage from our first marriages because what does not get healed is brought into the second marriage. Fun!

Journaling came in handy because it helped me to write all these feelings and frustrations out on paper where I could see them. You see them in a different way when they are on paper. Then voila! An answer hit me like a ton of bricks that was a win - win for everyone. And things smoothed out. We could not put a block on his phone to keep her from calling because of the kids. We read the book Boundaries by Cloud and Townsend and it was life changing; it is appropriate to put up boundaries to protect your marriage. Al was dealing with so many feelings and was being manipulated by her and that didn't help anything. It had been that way for years and when we talked to the Bishop and he finally realized what was happening things changed there too.

We dealt with the fear of blending finances and that took us a good 5 years to overcome with counseling, prayer, talking through things, arguing and a lot of frustration. And they had been through financial difficulties years before so it took time for him to trust me in taking part in the finances. He learned I was trustworthy and reliable with money but he still had triggers from his past. Therefore, we got to deal with one-sided control of the finances for a time. Also I was fearful to be left with nothing because of what he and I were going through. So my fist could stay pretty tight where money was concerned. It was huge for us to get to the point of buying a house with each other several years later. Right before we did, that is when we overcame so many of our insecurities.

You might think, why in the world did you two ever get married? These things didn't show up until after we were married. They were things that had been such traumas for the other in the first marriage and were not processed in the brain. They showed up in the second marriage to be healed, and they have been with lots of prayer and work. That is something huge if you can get it. We are out of balance when these types of things are present in our system. The body wants to heal.

Some people come into their first marriages and all kinds of triggers come up and you will scratch your head and say where did that anger come from or why did I just feel the way I felt? There is no reason for it! Well there sure may be. Something you went through earlier in life that was hurtful to you and may have never been processed is still there waiting to be cleared or talked about so the body can rebalance itself. Then that will no longer be a trigger for you.

The very thing I blamed my first husband for which was lack of communication was something that showed up big time for me to work out with Al. But it also showed up that he had some problems as well, even though it was in a different way. Communicating intimately and to the public are two different things. I am glad to say that has gotten much better and it adds a dimension to our relationship that I had not had before and I think he would say the same thing.

Kids and Divorce

I can't even begin to tell you how a divorce takes a toll on children and that could be several books on its own. People's circumstances are different. But I feel insecurity where marriage is concerned filters into their lives. If they were secure in your first marriage until things disintegrated that really puts a question in their minds about how stable they will be in their marriage or relationship.

My girls were so angry with me for several years. But I continued to try to repair what I could with them. As I learned things spiritually they would allow me to share with them and that was really positive. Some of Al's kids really wanted nothing to do with me for a time and some were ok. On his side, the same things happened. Some were very sweet and accepting. The thing the kids feel is that you are trying to take mom or dad's place and that is just not happening. That was the farthest thing in our minds.

You have to develop a thick skin being a parent or step parent. This didn't affect Al as much as it did me. He is so easy going it seemed to slide right off his back. My son accepted Al from the beginning, which was very helpful for me.

Holidays and Traditions

Another frustration with the kids have been holidays and traditions and trying to maintain what the kids grew up with. It wasn't too bad on my side but his ex and I had a lot of power struggles on this. I am happy to say things have worked out much better now. But those first few years trying to create our own traditions was pretty futile. The kids wanted and needed something to be the same.

Closure With Your Ex-Spouse

That is really important because I didn't get that with mine. Al did with his. It took me into the fourth year to realize that. Al gave me his blessing when I realized I needed to apologize and clear the air with my ex. I prayed about it and the counselor told me yes, if Al is ok with it, you should do it. The opportunity came and it totally changed everything. It was as if the stress that was there between us cleared and we could move on. That is best done before you get remarried and sometimes you will never be able to do that in person and you will just have to write a letter and not mail it.

Trying to plan your vacations is challenging. Because of scheduling conflicts and sharing the kids there were times we had to work together and reschedule time away occasionally. One time we ended up taking the ex-wife's dog with us on a trip to our timeshare and I resented that. I have had a lot of anger to work out regarding her. It's definitely a process.

How This Affected Me

Going through these things have taught me more courage and patience. And when someone says things about me that are untrue, I take that to Heavenly Father and let it go. I try not to worry about others' opinions of me as much. It has really taught me to hang in there in the tough times and not give up.

It's taught me to not be afraid to put up boundaries with people who are not good to you. Also to take care of your marriage and tend it carefully like a new garden. Weed it, fertilize it, water it and lovingly tend it daily.

It has taught me just because you failed once doesn't mean you will always be a failure. You can take the lessons learned and help other people with them. Time doesn't heal all things, because some things only Heavenly Father can heal. It was never about Al and I healing this. We could not have done anything we did without the Father's help and healing. His guidance and spirit was leading us and inspiring us about what the problems really were and what we needed to do to address them.

I have developed a compassion for people in blended families because it is hard! It is harder than if we had stayed in our first marriage! Yes, that is what I learned. If you can take anything away from this, take this. ***Stay put if you can.*** If there is not abuse or something that makes you or your kids feel unsafe, try to get help and get it early. Hardened anger is a force to be reckoned with. It is layers and layers built up. Think about mud that has hardened over time versus washing it off right after walking through the mud puddle. It takes a lot of effort to break through those layers, but with God anything is possible.

Don't Let The Sun Go Down On Your Anger

When you have had a disagreement, I learned to not let it linger. This was spoken of again in our course with Jimmy Evans. You know the kind of arguments I am speaking of, don't you? The kind where you each cling to the edge of the beds with your back towards each other and you don't give them the satisfaction of knowing you are awake or hurting over on your side. When you do that, you give the adversary a stronghold to put a wedge in between you and your spouse. I mean a deep wedge. The kind that questions if you were ever to be married to them to begin with or that maybe the first marriage wasn't as bad as it seemed. This anger that goes on and on is hardened anger and it can completely destroy a marriage. There have been times when I would get out of bed and we finished talking about something and then we could both sleep. Try not to address your concerns right at bedtime if at all possible. Even if you have to shelve it for another day and time at least your spouse knows it's going to get addressed and you are not just putting them off.

It Doesn't Happen Overnight

I was asked, how long did it take you all to make it through your difficulties? Let me be real honest here. Just in the last year we are overcoming our most difficult trials in our marriage. We prayed and asked for help and sought help, but it wasn't until the last month we have realized something that totally changed one important area of our lives. It has taken us personally 7 years. We have been married 7 ½ years. But all along the way things were improving.

One thing I have learned working in a church is that Heavenly Father has a lot of patience and confidence in you. Heavenly Father doesn't call people into callings because they are perfect or all-knowing, he calls them so they can grow or help others grow. The church would not run if he waited until people were perfect. The same goes for marriage. And if we are humble and teachable we can help each other grow.

Things started getting better after about the third year and then we took another nose-dive about the fourth year and we came up from there and here we are today. We had good times all along the way mixed in. I don't want you to think this was the marriage from hell but it sometimes felt like it because we had to learn how to deal and cope with things we had never been through before. I am so glad we stayed the course. We would have never known what we could have if we had given up.

My Internal Resources

Journaling worked very well for me. I began journaling in about 2005. Journaling helped me see what the real problems were and what the possible solutions could be. It helps you see the world around you and gives you a different perspective once you put things down on paper. Things come up in journaling that are so helpful to get you through hard times. And guess what? No one is there to judge you except yourself. Well, sometimes that can be brutal. But you can also soften the judgment on yourself because you see different things once they are out of your head and on paper.

I learned to rely on Heavenly Father more during these times. I felt those moments of encouragement and love, guidance and support. He would prompt people to call me when I was down and he would show me gently and tenderly where my flaws were. I love him and am so grateful he has blessed Al and I in our quest for a better marriage. My best friend, in her thirties married her husband who was a single father with 3 children. She told me of her story before I met Al and the challenges they faced for nine years. I watched her example and listened to her counsel. Little did I know I would get to work through some of those very things later down the road. Be open and learn from positive and successful people around you. My friend never made me feel judged. But she tried to tell me in the beginning about what we might encounter. She and her husband and their family have always been a wonderful support to Al and me.

The Importance of Mindset in Overcoming Adversity

This is huge and very critical. Pain can be very uncomfortable, but we must allow pain in our lives, recognize it and sit with it. Why not run? Because pain has lessons and messages for us, and if we allow it to, pain can instruct and teach us. It can help us grow. Pain can be our friend. Inquire of it and listen! Look at adversity as a gift. There is always a gift in it if we look closely enough. Sometimes we may not see it as we are going through it. But it will become apparent sooner or later.

5 Tips to Overcoming Adversity

1. First you have to choose success.

2. Keep company with positive and successful people. People who have been where you are and made it through. Don't keep company with people who fail where you want to succeed. That never works.

3. Calling upon your Father in heaven. If you could have someone who knew all your strengths and weaknesses overseeing your life and marriage, wouldn't it be important to call on them for help? Learn to listen and

follow promptings, or some people call it your gut. Follow those and things will work out. It doesn't always mean you won't go through problems but at the end of the day you will be happy, if you don't give up.

4. Don't give up when it gets hard. Stay the course because you never know what's on the other side of a trial!

5. Drop your unrealistic expectations of the relationship. Give it time. You are forging new ground here. Be patient. Learn about marriage. You would do as much for a new job and a marriage is a whole lot more important.

My Advice For Others

Again, commit to stay the course...hang in there. Don't put a timeline on healing.

I read this in *Boundaries for Marriage* by Cloud and Townsend. Sometimes a marriage has to go through some deep surgery to get better. Think of the surgery without commitment. What if the doctor decides to walk out of the operating room just before your heart bypass? You would surely die if they left before the operation that could have saved your life was finished. In marriage, God often wants to do that surgery that would save the life of your relationship. But how many times do we, the patients, hop off the table before it's complete because it's too painful? Commitment keeps the person on the table till the operation is finished.

Commitment builds security. When Al said to me, I am in this for the long haul and I am not going anywhere, something deep inside of me changed for the better. I felt he loved me enough and I was important enough to him not to abandon ship. I knew we were going to make it once he said that. It gave me hope. It changed the whole feel of our relationship as well.

Change takes time. Growth and change come with commitment. We stayed and worked through things and today we are at a much better place and I can see the wisdom of a loving and kind Heavenly Father in being quiet sometimes so we can ponder on our problems and seek for answers. Imagine a helicopter parent that is always and forever hovering over you and giving you the answers to all your problems. Don't we feel much stronger and better about ourselves when we work through things with minimal interference? Advice that is asked for is one thing. Do you feel capable if they are always giving you the answers? I don't. Clasp your partner's hand and hang on for the ride. It will get rough at times, but after it's done and you can look back you can say Wow! Look what we have come through and the people we have become!

And don't forget! Don't give up when it gets hard because your blessings are already on the way!

About the Author

Kim Roy

Connect with Kim on Facebook at www.fb.com/ LDSBlendedBlessed.

- Certified 'Marriage on the Rock" coach through Jimmy Evans Ministries.
- Certified in Bioenergetic Synchronization Technique (BEST) -- Master Level
- Currently certifying in Emotional Freedom Technique (EFT).

Kim Roy is a mother of five, step mother of six, grandmother to two-dozen and counting, in her second marriage going on eight years. She currently lives with her husband Al and their three dogs near Fort Worth, TX.

After her divorce 10 years ago, she committed to her own healing and to a closer relationship with Heavenly Father. He led Kim to her current husband Al, who was likewise committed to healing and spiritual growth. Not long after they married, Kim suffered what could have been a fatal fall that broke her left wrist and ended her career as a massage therapist.

Though most of her physical injuries have mended, that incident revealed other, deeper psychological and emotional hurts and pains that she had carried for much of her life. Thanks to the help of many, the love of the Lord and the knowledge and experience she's gained, Kim has been able to deal with those injuries. And she's come to learn that healing is a journey, not a destination.

"I now know my purpose in life is to help others along on their healing journey."

Stay Connected

Suzanne Doyle-Ingram – www.prominencepublishing.com

Maureen (Mo) Hagan – www.mohagan.com

Lani Gelera – www.fenixfallgirl.com

Mariam Griffith – mariamsells@sbcglobal.net

Nathalie Plamondon-Thomas – www.dnalifecoaching.ca

Kim Standeven – www.kimstandeven.com

Tasha Hughes – www.tashahughes.com

Pascale Hansen – www.stellarlifestrategies.com

Adrienne Blumberg – www.adrienneblumbergtherapy.com

Lynn Williams – www.lifestyleprotector.ca

Kim Roy – ldsblendedblessed@yahoo.com

Recommended Books

You Can Heal Your Life by Louise Hay

A New Earth by Eckhart Tolle

The Universe Has Your Back by Gabrielle Bernstein

When Bad Things Happen to Good People by Rabbi Harold S. Kushner

Oh the Places You'll Go by Dr. Seuss

Boundaries in Marriage by Henry Cloud and John Townsend

Feelings Buried Alive Never Die by Karol Truman

The Magic of Thinking Big by David J. Schwartz

About Prominence Publishing

Prominence Publishing is a boutique publishing company. We choose our clients carefully, so that we can produce the best books!

We work primarily with business professionals and entrepreneurs because we believe that becoming a published author and showcasing your expertise is one of the best ways to grow your business and gain massive exposure.

We offer writing programs, publishing packages, coaching, marketing services and more.

For more information, please visit www.prominencepublishing.com.

75751323R00098

Made in the USA
Columbia, SC
24 August 2017